SAINTS

AND

FEASTS

OF THE

CATHOLIC CALENDAR

VOLUME ONE OF FOUR

JANUARY - MARCH

SAINTS

AND

FEASTS

OF THE

CATHOLIC CALENDAR

VOLUME ONE OF FOUR

JANUARY - MARCH

FR. MICHAEL BLACK

Cover design by the author and Opus Creative Studio; Interior art by George Angelini, with permission, by Slawomir Miskow, with permission, by Opus Creative Studio, and courtesy of public domain images from the Städel Museum, Frankfurt am Main, the Getty Museum Open Content Program, and Wiki-Commons.

TABLE OF CONTENTS

Notes viii
Poem: Parade of Holiness x
Introduction 1

JANUARY		Page
1	Mary, the Mother of God	4
2	SS. Basil the Great & Gregory Nazianzen	5
3	The Most Holy Name of Jesus	7
4	St. Elizabeth Ann Seton	9
5	St. John Neumann	11
6	St. André Bessette	13
6	The Epiphany of the Lord (Moveable Feast)	14
7	St. Raymond of Peñafort	16
	The Baptism of the Lord (Moveable Feast)	17
13	St. Hilary	19
17	St. Anthony of the Desert	20
20	St. Fabian	22
20	St. Sebastian	23
21	St. Agnes	25
22	St. Vincent, Martyr	26
22	Day of Prayer for the Legal Protection of Unborn Children	28
23	St. Marianne Cope	30
24	St. Francis de Sales	32
25	Conversion of St. Paul	34
26	SS. Timothy & Titus	37

27	St. Angela Merici	39
28	St Thomas Aquinas	40
31	St. John Bosco	43

FEBRUARY **Page**

2	Presentation of the Lord	48
3	St. Blaise	50
3	St. Ansgar	52
5	St. Agatha	53
6	SS. Paul Miki & Companions	56
8	St. Jerome Emiliani	58
8	St. Josephine Bakhita	61
10	St. Scholastica	64
11	Our Lady of Lourdes	66
14	SS. Cyril & Methodius	67
17	Seven Holy Founders of the Servite Order	70
21	St. Peter Damian	72
22	Chair of St. Peter	75
23	St. Polycarp	77
27	St. Gregory of Narek	79

MARCH **Page**

3	St. Katharine Drexel	84
4	St. Casimir	87
7	SS. Perpetua & Felicity	89
8	St. John of God	91

9	St. Frances of Rome	94
17	St. Patrick	96
18	St. Cyril of Jerusalem	98
19	St. Joseph	100
23	St. Turibius of Mogrovejo	103
25	Annunciation of the Lord	105

LENT, HOLY WEEK & MOVEABLE FEASTS **Page**

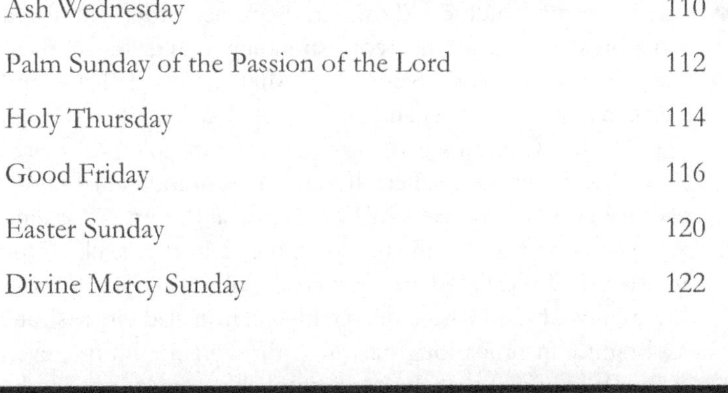

Ash Wednesday 110

Palm Sunday of the Passion of the Lord 112

Holy Thursday 114

Good Friday 116

Easter Sunday 120

Divine Mercy Sunday 122

A Parade of Holiness

NOTES ON VOLUME ONE AND THIS SERIES

- Many saints and blesseds are the official patrons of more than one place, activity, thing, or class of people. Many saints and blesseds are also, by custom or mere digital rumor, the unofficial patrons of various other places, activities, things, or classes of people. The saintly patronages cited herein are accurate but not exhaustive. Some more obscure saints lack any patronage at all.

- Spellings of saint and place names are often according to their original language but not exclusively so.

- The cover of Volume I shows, in clockwise order, simulated passport stamps, with their corresponding feast days, for Mary, the Mother of God, Saint Paul Miki, Saints Felicity and Perpetua, Saint Sebastian, and Saint Patrick. The design conveys the Church's geographical and chronological reach. As the reader immerses herself in the lives of individual saints, she will cross the borders of Europe, Asia, the Americas, and Africa. She will move up and down the centuries, walking the international terrain of the universal Church to briefly meet the friends of God whose deep faith and iron clad virtue shone so brightly in times long past and, through the liturgy, even today. It is hoped that the cover implicitly conveys that to be an informed Catholic is to be a wise, well-travelled, "two-thousand-year-old" person. An intentional Catholic is not just a citizen of the world as it is but of the world as it was and always will be.

- Although the word "feast" is commonly used indiscriminately to refer to any holy day, the Church uses more precise categories: *Solemnity*, *Feast, Memorial*, and *Optional Memorial.* On certain days of Lent and Advent, a *Memorial* has traditionally been referred to as a *Commemoration*. The Church does not, however, officially use the term *Commemoration* apart from All Souls Day. The liturgical designations cited herein are accurate, though not as fully elaborated as in an Ordo. The subtleties by which the Catholic liturgical calendar operates are not detailed.

- The dates of birth and of death of some saints are either totally unknown or disputed by different sources. The letter "c" stands for the Latin *circa*, "about," and is employed when the saint's specific dates are unknown. When a date is disputed among reputable sources, the date given in *Butler's Lives* is generally cited, although not always so.

- The "Catholic Calendar" of the title refers, more specifically, to the sanctoral calendar of the Roman Missal, Third Typical Edition, 2002 (English Language Edition 2011). Saint and feast days inserted into the universal sanctoral calendar subsequent to 2011 by the Congregation for Divine Worship and Discipline of the Sacraments are incorporated into this series through the end of 2021. The liturgical calendar of the United States Conference of Catholic Bishops, which adds some North American saints to the universal calendar, is normative for this series.

- Thousands of men and women have been canonized by the Congregation for the Causes of Saints and its predecessor Congregations. Many saints, however, date from the pre-Congregation era of the first millennium, when popular acclamation, local episcopal approbation, or long custom were sufficient to confer the title "saint." Only a small percentage of all these stars of holiness shine brightly enough to be included on the Church's universal calendar. It is precisely this constellation of "all-star" saints, and only those saints, who are presented in this series, rather than every single saint known to the Church's long history.

A PARADE OF HOLINESS

The path to God trod alone, without temptation or distraction,
No pilgrims stride aside unknown, spicing walk with conversation,
Quickens the soul's pace to God, on a road *sans* names and faces,
Hastening steps on a path unshod, a solemn journey of silent graces.

Yet to push the full plate away, gazing at a bounty untasted,
Bridling oneself from the freshest hay, renders creation wasted.
So while the solitary track, may aid the holy soul's survival,
Traveling without a pack rejects "It's the getting there, not the arrival."

The Church then offers each day, to her faithful a holy companion
To keep us from wandering away, travelers alone and abandoned.
In this parade of holiness, are saints with sweet sounding names,
Falling from lips harmonious, or in one easy syllable like "James."

Other saints have clumsier handles, eluding grip by the tongue,
All twisted knots and thick tangles, you grapple on every wrung.
Alas tricked by the mind, we think good those merely remembered
And misshapen names toss aside, to mind's oblivion surrendered.

An easy name clings to the brain, accessed quickly when requested,
Yet names going against the grain, lie dormant and sequestered.
It is folly to think a melodious name, musters most quickly in line,
Or to make the dubious claim, that smooth and greatness must entwine.

Let us now weave and meander, up and down our sacred year,
Where strange cognomes gerrymander, and sting the tender ear.
To courteously greet strangers, destined here to be friends
We must their multisyllabic dangers, avoid, master or amend.

Plodding through January's gloom, we spy Gregory Nazianzen.
Then a slave from Khartoum, a girl stolen by Muslim clansmen.
That's warm Josephine Bakhita, amid February's cold chills,
Whose journey from slavery to freedom, the beating heart stills.

Amid late March's Lenten days, Lima's Turibius of Mogrovejo,
While April's resurrecting rays, shine on a martyr known less so,
Fidelis of Sigmaringen, a Franciscan who for preaching fearless,
Surrendered his one possession: life, heroic and peerless.

In May's lengthening hours, the remote lepers' sole friend,
Like Hawaii's flowers, Damien DeVeuster, bursted love to the end.
With companions in Africa's east, a wicked chief their accuser
Charles Lwanga crowns this June feast, torched by an abuser.

In steamy July a Mohawk, honoring Siena's ascetic, so holy,
Face scarred by smallpox, and baptized Kateri, a lily bent lowly.
In scorching August an ancient bishop exiled, solid as a rock,
Eusebius of Vercelli finally reconciled, returned aged to his flock.

As September days move on, martyrs for Truth and Maria,
Andrew Kim Tae-gŏn, and companions, the pride of Korea.
Working in October's golden glow, appears a Franciscan brother,
Juan of Capistrano grace did sow, harvesting one soul after another.

Amid November's frosty nights, we mourn an Eastern victim,
Saint Josaphat, no last rites, his skull split by the vindictive.
In December's darkness a monk, vanished deep into the desert,
Iconoclasts Damascene debunked, wearing barely a hair shirt.

And so our merry group united, its destination reaches,
In spading faith with talk delighted, not in heavy speeches.
Conversing long with saints galore, we pierce religion's crust
Burnishing gold through our rapport, what seemed before mere rust.

That unknown day our long walk ends, traveling days are done,
A sun lit basilica, full of friends, bowing deep, a deathless Son.
Stunned hearts at the sight will leap, as shafts divine beam like the sun,
Toward reunions sweet, eyes aweep, our legs break from walk to run.

Yet over our shoulders we'll cry out, thanks to all those saints,
Behind us now singing songs devout, as we approach St. Peter's gate.
Banners waving, exuberant cheer, seated high atop life's rich parade,
They bathed us in grace one full year, a sacred cavalcade in virtue arrayed.

M.B.

INTRODUCTION

These pages profile the theological bone breakers, the verbal flame throwers, the ocean crossers, the heart-melters, and the sweet-chanting virgin-martyrs who populate the liturgical calendar of the Catholic Church.

Here is the black robe in his canoe, rowing alone on a placid lake as darkness falls on the rim of the world. Here is the bearded, Dark Ages bishop, plodding through the dark forests of the north when he is suddenly felled by a flurry of pagan clubs. Here is the highly civilized Roman patrician who bows his head to receive the waters of baptism, serves his city as a bishop, and then kneels solemnly to be executed, his white toga stained with his warm, red blood. Here is the serene, wordless, monk seated in his damp cave, high in the cliff face, gazing over the endless desert below. Here is the electrifying Dominican preacher standing on a wooden platform in the medieval town square, thundering, "I'm-going-to-light-my-hair-on-fire–WATCH-ME-BURN!" And here is the missionary Irish scholar-monk riding the waves of the Channel like a cork in his oarless boat, leaving behind his rainy home to sow the seeds of a new Europe, one monastery at a time.

The incandescent and to-be-discovered Marian Church of heaven and the oh-so-human flawed Petrine Church on earth are the two charged poles between which crackles an arc of holiness. Love of Christ and love of Mary electrify the Church, our mother and object of faith. We need no warlocks, fairies, or superheroes to power our imagination. We have high drama enough in our Church's saints to make the mind wander to a land far, far away, or to a shrine just one town over.

Volume I of *Saints and Feast Days of the Catholic Calenda*r tries to convey, in a condensed fashion, just a touch of the theodrama powering the triumphs and the tragedies, the victories and the defeats, the hidden perseverance and the great public gestures of the greatest men and women who have ever lived.

JANUARY

Looking back - looking forward

January 1: Solemnity of Mary, the Mother of God

Solemnity; Holy Day of Obligation (in USA: unless a Saturday or Monday)
Eighth Day of the Octave of Christmas; Liturgical Color: White

No one knew Jesus like Mary

No one falls in love with a nature. We fall in love with a person. A woman loves a man, not mankind. And a mother pinches the pudgy little cheeks of a newborn baby, not the cheeks of a newborn nature. Saint Mary gave birth to a little person, a baby, unlike any other. In that little person, a human nature united with a divine nature at the moment of conception. So Mary was the mother of the person Jesus, and the person Jesus had two natures, one fully human and the other fully divine. Saint Mary was, then, the mother of Jesus' human nature *and* of His divine nature. She was both the mother of a man and the mother of God.

Two false extremes must be identified and rejected here. Jesus was not really and truly only a God who just faked being a man. Nor was He really a man who just pretended to be a God. The Son of God did not wear a fleshy human mask to conceal the radiance of His real divine face. And Jesus the man did not wear His divinity like a cloak that He could remove from His shoulders when He walked in the door. Jesus was fully God and fully man in a mystery of faith we call the hypostatic union. And because a woman is a mother to a person, not just to a nature, Mary is the mother of God. This has been the constant doctrine of the Catholic Church since the Council of Ephesus in 431 A.D.

Saint Mary has many titles under which we honor her. Today's Solemnity commemorates the utterly unique, and unrepeatable, bond she shared with Jesus, a bond no other saint can claim. Jesus and Mary probably even looked very much alike, as hers was the only human DNA in His body. What a beautiful thing that our God did not float down from heaven on a golden pillow. How good that He was not forged from a fiery anvil. How right that He did not ride to earth on a thunderbolt. Jesus could not redeem what He did not assume. So it was fitting that He was born like all of us—from a mom. We honor Mary today for her vocation as mother. If she had disappeared from the pages of the Gospels after giving birth to Jesus, she still would have fulfilled her role in salvation history. She was obedient. She was generous. She allowed God to use her, body and soul, to write the first chapter of man's true story, the story of the Church. Like all true stories, the person comes first. A life is lived, and the book comes later.

God's Mother gives us our mother, Holy Mother Church, who washes our souls in the saving waters of baptism, adopting us into God's family. The Motherhood of Mary gives the world Jesus. Jesus gives us the Church. The Church then brings us into God's family where Mary is our mother, Jesus our brother, and God our Father. This is the family of the Church. What pride to be members of so noble a family!

O Mother of God, you birthed the one who created all. How beautiful the mystery. How exalted your vocation that precedes and makes possible the Apostles' own vocations. At home you bounced on your knee the one who spins the world on His finger. Help us start this new year with wonder more than resolutions, with eternal gratitude more than mundane goals.

January 2: Saints Basil the Great and Gregory Nazianzen, Bishops and Doctors

St. Basil: 329–379; St. Gregory: c. 329–390

Memorial; Liturgical Color: White

Patron Saints of Russia, monks, hospital administrators, and poets

Obvious truths are hard to explain, but smart theologians can explain them

The persecution of the Church in the first few centuries, sometimes aggressive, more typically passive, starved her skinny biblical frame of nourishment. When the Emperor Constantine legalized Christianity in 313 A.D., the Church's bones finally stretched, grew, and added muscle on muscle. Churches opened. Bishops preached. Schools taught. Theologians wrote. And, most significantly, Councils met. Three hundred years after Jesus Christ ascended into heaven, these large gatherings of bishops and theologians sought to end theological confusion, to settle thorny questions, and to establish a standard Christian doctrine. In the vast halls and churches of these councils, the great cast of theologians of the fourth century put their prodigious talents on full display. We commemorate two of the greatest of these bishops and theologians in today's memorial.

Saints Basil and Gregory lived so long ago, were so prolific, and played such crucial roles in so many areas of Church life, that they could each be remembered for any number of contributions to liturgy, theology, ecclesiology, Church history, monasticism, and even popular customs, especially in the Orthodox East. Yet perhaps their greatest contributions were as theologians who defined, fundamentally and decisively, what the word Trinity actually means; how Jesus is both fully God and fully man; and how the Holy Spirit is related to God the Father. Such definitions and distinctions may seem technical, abstract, or remote. But it is always the most obvious things—the most necessary things—that are the most difficult to explain. Why do things fall down instead of up? Why does the sun rise in the east instead of the west? Why are there seven days in a week instead of nine?

The most fundamental doctrines of our faith, understood now as perennial, were not always perennial. They originated in the minds of certain people at certain times in certain places. To today's saints we owe the decisive words that the Holy Spirit "proceeds" from the Father and the Son. These words fall simply and familiarly from our lips. But the word "proceeds" was the fruit of intense thought and prayer. The Father generated the Son, but the Holy Spirit "proceeds" from them both. Interesting. Dozens of millions of Catholics say reflexively every Sunday that the second Person of the Trinity is "consubstantial" with the Father. Not equal in origin. Not equal in role. But "consubstantial," or equal in nature. Thank you, Saints Basil and Gregory! Thank you, great Bishops and Doctors of the early Church! Thank you for pulling aside the veil of mystery for a peek into the Godhead.

Without the teachings of the fourth century on the Trinity and Christ, there would be no Christmas trees. Think about that. Why celebrate the Christ child if He were not God? But He is God. So carols are composed, mangers are set up, lights are hung, and gifts are exchanged. Culture happens, culture flourishes, when theology makes sense. Thank you, Saints Basil and Gregory, for… everything!

O noble Bishops and Doctors Basil and Gregory, we ask for your continued intercession to enlighten our minds and to remove the dark shadows that cause confusion. Assist us to recognize that good theology understands God as He understands Himself. When you gave us good teaching, you gave us God. We seek nothing more.

January 3: The Most Holy Name of Jesus

Optional Memorial; Liturgical Color: White

Names are powerful, and none is more powerful than Jesus

Mary and Joseph did not sit across from each other at the kitchen table in the evenings debating a name for their child. They didn't flip through the pages of a book of saints or bounce ideas off of their friends and family. The baby's name was chosen for them by God Himself. They were just taking orders. The Archangel Gabriel announced to Mary, "And now, you will conceive in your womb and bear a son, and you will name him Jesus" (Lk 1:31). And Joseph had a dream in which the angel told him, "...you are to name him Jesus, for he will save his people from their sins" (Mt 1:21). The Gospel of Luke further relates that "After eight days had passed, it was time to circumcise the child; and he was called Jesus, the name given by the angel before he was conceived in the womb" (Lk 2:21). Jesus was named eight days after Christmas, January 3.

The New Testament is filled with incidents where the name of Jesus is invoked to drive out devils, cure illnesses, and perform miracles. The Holy Name is explicitly exalted by Saint Paul: "...at the name of Jesus every knee should bend, in heaven and on earth and under the earth" (Phil 2:10). Jesus reinforces the power of His own name in St. John's Gospel: "...if you ask anything of the Father in my name, he will give it to you" (Jn 16:23).

"Jesus" was the given name of the Son of Mary, while "Christ" was a title. "Christ" is the Greek form of the Hebrew "Messiah," meaning the "Anointed One." "Jesus the Christ" was the original formula for describing the Son of Mary. But over time, "The Christ" became simply "Christ," as if it were His last name. The name of the God of the Old Testament was holy, not to be written out, nor to be casually spoken. Invoking "Yahweh" could be so egregious a sin as to provoke the tearing of the hearer's shirt in protest and repentance. Jewish law on God's holy name is enshrined in the second commandment: "Thou shalt not take the name of the Lord Thy God in vain." This commandment prohibited the swearing of false oaths, that is, calling upon God as your witness and then making false statements. The opposite of a solemn oath is invoking the name of God to damn someone or something: a curse—the inversion of a blessing.

Saint Bernardine of Siena, an electrifying Franciscan preacher of the early fifteenth century, was the saint who most spread devotion to the Holy Name of Jesus. He ingeniously depicted the Holy Name with the well-known monogram "IHS," derived from the Greek letters forming the word "Jesus." In the sixteenth century, the Jesuits built on this tradition and utilized the "IHS" to embellish their churches, even making it the emblem of their Society. The mother church of all Jesuit churches, in Rome, is officially named in honor of the Most Holy Name of Jesus, although its name is commonly shortened to simply "The Jesus."

There is raw power in the name Jesus. It makes polite company cringe. It divides families. It floats across the dinner table, letting everyone know exactly where you stand. A comfortable, vague euphemism like "the man upstairs" or "the big guy" just won't do. "Jesus" does not convey an idea that everyone can interpret as they wish. It's someone's name. And that someone taught, suffered, died, rose from the dead, ascended into heaven, and is seated at the right hand of the Father in heaven.

Some people don't like their names and seek to legally change them or to use a nickname instead. Names convey meanings. "Thor" sounds like a mythical god carrying a hammer, "Vesuvius" sounds like a boiling volcano about to erupt, and a "ziggurat" sounds like a zig-zaggy desert temple. The name "Jesus" sounds like a God-man beyond reproach. A child, when once asked to define love, said that "when someone loves you, the way they say your name is different. Your name is safe in their mouth." The Holy Name of Jesus should be safe in our mouths even when we're not receiving Holy Communion.

Son of Mary, may our same tongues that receive Your Holy Body and Blood prepare themselves for Your visit by saying Your Holy Name with great reverence. And may we not refrain from invoking that same Holy Name in our daily conversations with all whom we meet.

January 4: Saint Elizabeth Ann Seton, Religious (U.S.A.)

1774–1821

Optional Memorial; Liturgical Color: White

Patron Saint of Catholic schools, widows, loss of parents

She had it all, lost it all, and then found it all again

In late 1803, Elizabeth Ann Seton, with her husband, left the United States for Italy, as a confident, high-born, wealthy, educated Yankee Protestant. She returned in June 1804, bankrupt, a widow, burning with love for the Holy Eucharist, tenderly devoted to Mary, and with the heart of a Roman Catholic. She was received into the Church the next year. Her upper-class friends and family abandoned her out of anti-Catholic spite.

Our saint was an unexpected convert. She was, well into adulthood, a serious U.S. Episcopalian. She loved the Lord. She loved the Bible. She loved to serve the poor and the sick. Her excellent Episcopalian upbringing provided sufficient preparation for not being Episcopalian any longer. She took that faith as far as it could go. She probably never suspected her faith was lacking until she experienced the abundance of Catholicism.

After her husband died of tuberculosis in Pisa Italy, Elizabeth and her daughter were taken in by family friends from nearby Livorno. In God's providence, this Italian family lived their faith with relish. Elizabeth was not only consoled and cared for by them in her grief but also saw how engrossing their faith was. The longer she stayed in Italy, the more its Catholic atmosphere enveloped her. She wept at Italians' natural devotion to Mary. She wondered at the beauty of a Corpus Christi procession through the narrow streets of her town. She understood the Holy Father's link to the early Apostles with clarity. And so she came to see the gaps in her native religion. She hadn't noticed them before. Having seen the real thing with her own

ST. ELIZABETH ANN SETON

January 4

"The gate of heaven is very low; only the humble can enter it."

eyes, she knew that she held a replica in her hands. The real presence of Christ in Catholicism is often understood only after a real absence is felt in non-Catholic Christianity.

After her conversion, Elizabeth spent the rest of her short life dedicated to Catholic education. She started a Congregation of sisters in Maryland that taught girls, especially poor girls who could not afford an education. She was the first of tens of thousands of teaching sisters to operate Catholic schools in the United States. She is rightly considered in the United States as the foundress of Catholic parochial education. Besides her husband, she also lost two of her five children during her lifetime. She struggled, like all founders, to build up her Congregation. But her intelligence, charm, and drive paid off. Her Order thrived and thrives still. The Daughters of Charity of St. Vincent de Paul gather each year on this feast near her tomb inside an immense Basilica in Northern Maryland to thank God for their foundress, for a life so well lived.

Saint Elizabeth Ann Seton, help us overcome the alienation of family due to our religious convictions. Aid us in persevering through the hardships of illness and death, and give us the same zeal for souls that you showed toward your students, seeing in each one the image of God.

January 5: Saint John Neumann, Religious (U.S.A.)

1811–1860

Memorial; Liturgical Color: White

Patron Saint of Catholic education

He gave of himself until there was nothing left to give

Today's saint worked like a mule. He studied, he wrote, he prayed, he preached, he traveled, he built, he founded, he guided, he taught. And then one day, carrying construction plans for his Cathedral in Philadelphia to an office, he died in the street. He had worked himself to death. He was forty-eight years old.

Saint John Neumann was born in Central Europe in what is today the Czech Republic. Like many people born in small countries, he had to learn more than his native tongue in order to become a success. But Saint John outdid himself. He learned seven languages in addition to his native Czech. He had a gift. Yet he found it hard to find a bishop to ordain him after he had completed his theological studies. He wrote to numerous bishops throughout Europe and to one on the other side of an ocean he had never seen. The other-side-of-the-ocean bishop wrote back: If you can get here, I'll ordain you. Saint John got there and was ordained in 1836 by Bishop John Dubois of New York, himself a transplant from Paris, France.

He was assigned to rural areas in Upstate New York and was outstanding in his zeal for souls. But the isolation was a burden, and he felt the need for priestly community. So he joined the Redemptorist Order and began many years of priestly service in Maryland. His intelligence, ability to preach and hear confessions in multiple languages, extraordinary work ethic, life of poverty, good nature, and general holiness were traits that all observed and all admired. He was named the fourth Bishop of Philadelphia in 1852. The city's growth was exploding, especially its Catholic population of immigrants. Saint John threw himself into his work with no concern for his own well-being. He was a tornado of apostolic activity. He was everywhere and did everything. The Church benefitted and grew at an extraordinary pace. But Saint John's only gear was overdrive, and he did not personally benefit. Zeal for His house consumed him, and zeal for His house killed him. Yet that is probably the way he wanted it.

Saint John was buried in a Redemptorist Church in Philadelphia, and his reputation for holiness quickly spread after his death. The faithful asked. The faithful received. The miracles were documented, and Philadelphia had its saint. Saint John Neumann was canonized by Pope Saint Paul VI in 1977, an immigrant who was the first male American citizen to be raised to the altars.

Saint John, you left home and family to toil in the remote regions of the United States for the sake of the Gospel. Your tireless dedication to the needs of the Church is an inspiration to all, especially priests. Enkindle in the hearts of all priests the same fire of love that burned in your own.

January 6: Saint André Bessette, Religious (Canada; U.S.A.)

1845–1937

Optional Memorial (Canada & U.S.A.); Liturgical Color: White

Patron Saint of family caregivers

He loved the Word of God, though he could not read

Saint Paul teaches in his letter to the Romans that faith comes by hearing. It's a good thing it doesn't come only by reading. Until modern times, a relatively small percentage of the population has been able to read. Today's saint had faith enough to move mountains, yet if he looked at the page of an open book, he saw only impenetrable symbols. André Bessette was functionally illiterate. His faith did not come by reading or study. It came by hearing, by watching, by praying, by listening, and by reflecting.

As Catholics, we are not a people of the Book. We are a people of the Word. And that Word is an idea and a person long before it is a script. "In the beginning was the Word...and the Word became flesh," Saint John's Gospel begins. Our faith would live and thrive even if the Bible had never been compiled. The Church is a living Word. Saint André's life witnesses to the primacy of the living Word over the written Word.

Saint André was the eighth child born into a large and desperately poor family from Quebec, Canada. Alfred was his baptismal name. His father died in a logging accident and his mother of tuberculosis by the time he was 12. The many children had to be dispersed to friends and relatives. Our saint then spent the next thirteen years doing manual labor, including factory and farm work, throughout the Northeastern United States. After he had wandered enough, he wandered back home by age 25. His perceptive parish priest noted his generosity of spirit and deep faith. He recommended the young man to the Congregation of the Holy Cross in Montreal, sending Alfred to them with an almost unbelievably prophetic note stating: "I am sending you a saint."

Alfred took the name of this same parish priest, André, and after much difficulty was allowed to join the Congregation as a brother. He was given the unremarkable task of minding the door of a boys' school, where he welcomed guests, delivered mail, and ran errands.

But then something happened. And happened again. And then still again. Sick people who came to visit him were cured by his touch and his prayers. Brother André insisted it was God and Saint Joseph.

Thus began a many decades-long ministry to the sick of Canada who sought out his healing touch. The lines of sick people became so long that he could no longer do his job at the school door. He attended to people all day long. He became famous for all the right reasons. He built a modest shrine to Saint Joseph on a hill. The shrine became very popular and grew until it became, and still is today, the most dominant structure in all of Montreal. Our saint did not live to see it completed. But he lived so long and so well that one million people filed past his casket when he died. He edified people not by his learning but by his healing and by the warm humanity that animated it.

Saint André, you healed the sick and found time to attend to all who came to you. You encouraged those who sought you to confess their sins and to go to Mass. Intercede for all believers so that we see in Jesus our divine physician, healer of soul and body.

January 6: The Epiphany of the Lord

January 6 or the first Sunday after January 1 where this feast is not a Holy Day of Obligation
Solemnity; Liturgical Color: White/Gold

Catholicism did multiculturalism before anyone else

The Feast of the Epiphany has traditionally been considered more theologically important than almost any other Feast Day, including Christmas. The early Christians had only Scripture, not the wealth of tradition we have today, to guide them in marking the great events of the life of Christ. So Holy Week and Easter, the Baptism of the Lord, Pentecost, and the Epiphany jumped off the pages of Scripture as great events which merited celebration. These few dates became fixed points on the calendar and were later surrounded over the centuries with numerous other feasts and saints' days.

Two lessons from the visit of the Magi are worth considering. The first is that the wise men's gifts were given *after* Christmas. Many

Catholic cultures preserve the ancient tradition of giving gifts on the Epiphany, not on Christmas itself. This tradition separates the birth of Christ from gift giving. When these two things—the birth of Christ and the giving of gifts—are collapsed into the same day, it causes some confusion of priorities, and the birth of Christ never wins. Waiting to exchange gifts until January 6 lets the Child God have the stage to Himself for a day. It makes people, especially children, wait—a rarity in the modern Western world. Postponing gift-giving until January 6 makes for a long, leisurely Christmas season and has the benefit of tradition and good theology as well.

Another great lesson from the Magi is more theological—that a true religion must be true for everyone, not just for some people. Truth is not geographical. It climbs over borders. Truth by its nature conquers untruth. The Magi are the first non-Jews, or Gentiles, to worship Christ. They tell us that the mission field of Christ is the whole world, not just the Holy Land. The Church is forever bound, then, to teach, preach, and sanctify the world over.

The Magi crack everything open. The true God and His Church must light a fire in Chinese souls, Arab souls, African souls, and South American souls. This may take until the end of time, but Christianity has time on its side. The Magi give personal testimony to the universality of the Church, one of its four marks. The Epiphany is the start of the multi-cultural, multi-lingual, multi-ethnic, and faith-united society that the Catholic Church envisions as the only source of true human unity. Catholicism started multiculturalism and diversity without sacrificing unity and truth.

Balthasar, Caspar, and Melchior, your minds were prepared to receive a greater truth. You give an example of holy curiosity, of pilgrimage by light to light. When you discovered your treasure, you laid down your gifts in homage. May our search also find. May our pilgrimage also end in truth.

January 7: Saint Raymond of Peñafort, Priest

c. 1175–1275

Optional Memorial; Liturgical Color: White

Patron Saint of canon lawyers and medical record librarians

He wove scripture and the law into a harmonious tapestry

Today's saint lived numerous lives inside of his one hundred years on earth. He was an intellectual prodigy who was teaching university-level philosophy by the age of twenty and who took degrees in civil and canon law from the premier law university of the time—Bologna. While in Bologna, he likely came to know the founder of a new religious Order who had also moved there and who would later die there—Saint Dominic de Guzman. The example of the Dominicans led Father Raymond to exchange the diocesan priesthood for the Dominicans.

Saint Raymond's abilities and holiness were such that everyone seemed to want him in their service. Kings and Popes and Bishops and Orders all had plans on how to utilize him best. He was called to the Pope's service to make the great contribution for which he is still known today, the organization of a huge compendium of Church law which served as the basic reference for canon lawyers until the early twentieth century. Exhausted by his three years of effort on this project, he returned in middle age to his native Barcelona.

But his life of quiet and prayer did not last long. He was shocked to learn from Dominicans sent to him from Bologna that he had been elected the second successor to Saint Dominic as the Master General of the Dominican Order. He served his Order well and dutifully as Master General but not long. He resigned due to old age when he was 65. But there was still a lot of life left to live. Saint Raymond's activities in his old age included efforts to try to convert the Muslims then occupying Spain, his rejection of an episcopal appointment, the establishment of theology and language schools dedicated to converting Muslims, and his probable personal encouragement of the young Thomas Aquinas to write an apologetic work directed at non-Catholics, the *Summa contra Gentiles*.

Saint Raymond's life shows an admirable synthesis of traditional piety and devotion, service to the Church, obedience to his superiors, love of theology, dedication to his Order, and respect and love for the law.

To know, love, and follow the law is not contrary to charity. When kept, the law promotes charity and protects the weak, the poor, and the ignorant from being taken advantage of. It takes very smart and holy people to protect simple people and bad people from themselves. Saint Raymond was smart and holy. He laid his gifts at the altar of God, and God used those gifts splendidly.

Saint Raymond, teach us to see the law of God and the law of the Church as one harmonious law meant to foster true communion among men and true communion between God and men. May God's law be our law. And may the law never be an obstacle to true love and devotion.

Sunday after January 6: The Baptism of the Lord

First Century

Sunday after January 6 or the Monday after the Epiphany

Feast; Liturgical Color: White/Gold

He humbly bowed His head as an example, not because He was imperfect

Who would not want a doctor who, before he cuts, lifts his shirt a little, shows his own scar, and says to the patient, "I had the same. It's going to be alright!" What soldier would not be just a little braver, stand a little taller, seeing medals for valor on his commander's uniform? We want our heroes, our leaders, and our guides to lead through personal example. To have been there. To have done that. And we want our Savior to do the same. To empathize. To participate. To identify. To accompany. Actions resonate more than words.

Our sinless God "became" sin, in the words of Saint Paul. Jesus identifies with sin but never sinned. Jesus carries sin but is not a sinner. Why? Because to become sin is to become man. In order for God to enter into human reality, He had to identify with all that sin entails. God wanted to stand with us shoulder to shoulder. He did not fake becoming man but really became man. And if God came to forgive sins and sinners, and to shed His blood for them on the cross, He had to bear the burden they bore yet retain His perfection.

The Baptism of Christ
Luca Cambiaso

This is why our sinless God was baptized on today's feast. God lays to the side His perfection and dignity and bows His head in the dirty waters of the Jordan River. He lined up with sinners to receive in humility what He did not need, to attend a school whose subjects He had mastered. Our God knew the value of empathy. He knew the power of example. And He knew that His ministry to mankind had to start not on a golden throne but in the mud with other men just trying to start again and again and again.

The fullness of the Holy Trinity, first revealed subtly at the Annunciation, is present and spoken for at the Lord's baptism. The Holy Spirit, in the form of a dove, hovers. The voice of God the Father intones His favor over His Son. And the Son enters into the essential Christian pact with man—I will become like you so that you can become like me. Sins will be taken away through water and blood. I will suffer for your benefit. This is the promise. And the Church's priests will carry on the baptizing, forgiving, and consecrating until the sun sets for the last time. God comes to us most intensely through the Sacraments. Jesus' actions prove this.

O Lord, You are not remote. You know sin but are not a sinner. Help us to renew our baptism through a frequent reception of confession and the Holy Eucharist. By receiving one, we strengthen the others. By receiving You, we receive God Himself.

January 13: Saint Hilary, Bishop and Doctor

c. 310–c. 367

Optional Memorial; Liturgical Color: White

Patron Saint of lawyers

A pagan discovers Christ, converts, and then suffers for Him

Today's saint was born a pagan, to pagans, in a pagan city. But his broad and deep education brought him into contact with Holy Scripture, where he found the truth he did not know he was seeking. He became a Catholic through reading. He was to then spend his adult life defending Catholic truth with his pen. The convert converted others and preserved the orthodoxy of the Nicene Creed against the Arian heresy. Saint Athanasius called Saint Hilary a "trumpet" of orthodoxy against theological error.

Saint Hilary was elected the Bishop of Poitiers, France, about 350. His learning and intelligence placed him at the center of the violent theological battles of the fourth century. The Council of Nicea in 325 had left some theological definitions open to incorrect interpretation. A man named Arius caused immense confusion by just such misinterpretation. Arius argued that the words of the Nicene Creed meant that Jesus was less than God the Father, that Jesus had a beginning in time, and that Jesus was of like substance to the Father, not of the same substance. Saint Hilary was the first theologian from the West, as opposed to the more theologically mature theologians from Egypt, Asia Minor, and the Middle East, to see what a grave threat Arianism was.

Saint Hilary spent the better part of his adult life studying, writing, and arguing to ensure that the Nicene Creed was understood and adhered to throughout the Church. He was even sent into exile by the Emperor for not conforming his views to Arian teachings. But he used his time in exile to read and write extensively, eventually becoming such a thorn in the side of the Emperor that he restored Hilary to his diocese. Saint Hilary went on to attend various synods of bishops in an effort to maintain the truth of the Nicene Creed against determined opposition at the highest levels.

Hilary's life proves that good theology matters. Bad theology easily leads to bad worship, bad morality, and the decline of true Christian community. To disrupt or correct bad theology is to disrupt or correct bad community. And it is sometimes the obligation of the Church to break up false ideas of the church, of marriage, of family, of government, etc. When certain things are built up, their opposites inevitably are broken up. Saint Hilary knew all of this. He knew that bad theology was not just bad in and of itself but that it also had negative repercussions in the lived reality of the Church. When Saint Hilary defended theological truth, he defended many other truths as well.

Saint Hilary, through reading and study, you came to love the truths of the Catholic faith. Your love then showed itself in your willingness to suffer for that truth. Help us to know, love, and serve God by knowing, loving, and serving the instrument of His truth on earth—the Catholic Church.

January 17: Saint Anthony of the Desert, Abbot

251–356

Memorial; Liturgical Color: White

Patron Saint of butchers, skin diseases, gravediggers, and swine

A solitary monk trades the world for the desert sands

Many extraordinary people who live heroic, path-breaking lives remain unknown to posterity for one simple reason—no one writes their biography. How many other saints, heroes, and martyrs would be known to mankind if just one witness to their actions had put pen to paper! Just one author is needed to introduce a great man to subsequent generations. Today's saint may have been forgotten forever—and may have wanted to remain unknown. But a talented and famous contemporary of his wrote what he knew. Saint Athanasius, the provocative champion of orthodoxy at the Council of Nicea, wrote a short biography of his fellow Egyptian, *The Life of Saint Anthony the Great*. Saint Athanasius' work was so widely shared, and so often translated, that it was never lost to history. It has preserved Saint Anthony's memory down to the present.

The first three centuries of the Church saw sporadic persecutions of Christianity, which at times turned vicious. These spasms of violence against Christians produced a large class of martyrs, many of whose last words and sufferings were recorded in official Roman judicial documents or in the written testimonies of witnesses. As

Christianity was legalized at the start of the fourth century, martyrdom ceased to be the primary form of Christian witness. A new form of radical Christian discipleship emerged—the witness of total isolation, fasting, prayer, and penance of the desert fathers. These monks retreated into remote places to lead solitary lives of dedication to Christ. Foremost among these desert fathers was Saint Anthony of the Desert. He was not the first ascetic, but he was one of the first to take the radical decision to retreat into the desert.

Saint Anthony had money and property as a young man. But upon hearing at Mass the words of Christ to the rich young man to "...go, sell what you have and give to the poor, and you will have treasures in heaven," Anthony decided to seek not silver or bronze but pure gold. He sold his goods, he removed himself from all temptation except those intrinsic to human nature, he battled the devil, he fasted, he prayed, and he even actively sought martyrdom. He became famous for being holy. Saint Anthony preceded Saint Benedict by two hundred years. He offers us an example of being a monk outside of a community of fellow monks in a monastery. He sought Christ alone while living alone. Alone in the desert, without family, community, or money, listening to the howling winds at night. Alone to the world, he clung to the only person who truly mattered—God Himself.

Saint Anthony's path of holiness is both radical and refined. It is for few people to walk. But he was the first to walk it so well. Anthony shows us that being alone, stripped of all worldly concerns, is a sort of rehearsal for death, where we will meet God alone, every last thread tying us to the world having been cut.

Saint Anthony, we ask your intercession to help us cling to God alone. Help us to strip ourselves of those needs and concerns which stuff our lives from morning to night. Help us not to be distracted from the one thing, the only thing, the last thing—God Himself.

January 20: Saint Fabian, Pope and Martyr

c. 200–250

Optional Memorial; Liturgical Color: Red

Patron Saint of Rome

The popes of the third century knew how to die

In the present-day suburbs of Rome, tour buses navigate winding, narrow, tree-lined roads to carry modern pilgrims to the Catacombs of St. Callixtus. The pilgrims descend a steep staircase until they find themselves in a vast, dark, underground space. The pilgrims slowly walk by early Christian graffiti blanketing the walls to their right and to their left. Marble scraps of early Christian tombstones have etched upon them Greek and Latin epigraphs briefly describing whom they honor. In 1850 an archaeologist working in the St. Callixtus Catacombs discovered, incredibly, just such a small chunk of marble with the following simple epitaph: "Fabian, Bishop, Martyr." The epitaph confirmed the tradition that Fabian's lifeless body was carried in procession to these Catacombs shortly after his death in 250 A.D. In the early 1700s, Pope Fabian's relics were transferred to the nearby Church of Saint Sebastian, where they can be found today.

According to Eusebius of Caesarea, who wrote a detailed history of the Church about fifty years after Pope Fabian's time, Fabian was a layman who went to Rome after the death of the previous pope. He was elected Bishop of Rome due to a miraculous sign. In other words, Fabian did not strive to his high office. He did not seek to be important. He accepted his role in the full knowledge that it could lead to big trouble for him. And that trouble eventually found him.

A third-century letter of Saint Cyprian to the deacons and priests of Rome confirms the virtuous life and courageous death of Pope Fabian. Fabian reigned as Pope for fourteen years before being martyred in 250 A.D. The Roman Emperor Decius was his killer. Decius' persecution was vicious but not universal. He tried to kill the body of the Church by cutting off the head, and so sought the Pope's blood. But Decius' ambitious project was never realized. About sixty-five years later, one of Decius' successors, Constantine, would legalize Christianity, bringing to an end almost three hundred years of on-again, off-again persecution.

We can only imagine what it would be like today if the Pope were to be imprisoned and killed by the Prime Minister of Italy. Imagine the outcry! A secular power actively persecuting a religious leader! Yet perhaps such events are not so unimaginable. Pope Saint John Paul II was shot, and almost killed, in 1981, probably due to dark communist forces rooted in Eastern Europe. Assassins still exist, and popes are still their targets.

Pope Fabian's martyrdom shows why the Church survived its early and vicious persecutions—it had leaders who knew how to die. Great deaths don't follow shallow lives. The early popes didn't give up or give in. They didn't renounce the faith. They were fearless. They felt the cold, sharp metal of a knife against their neck and stood firm. A religious society with such models of courage in its highest ranks had to survive. And it did survive. We are living proof of that.

Saint Fabian, your papal death proved to the faithful that their leaders personally accepted what they demanded of others. Slaves, prisoners, women, outcasts, and popes all died for the faith. Help us, Fabian, to be further links in the Church's long chain of Christian witnesses.

January 20: Saint Sebastian, Martyr

Late Third Century

Optional Memorial; Liturgical Color: Red

Patron Saint of athletes, soldiers, and victims of the plague

A Roman soldier makes a rugged convert and stoic martyr

The Crucifixion of Jesus Christ and the Annunciation of the Archangel Gabriel to the Virgin Mary are the most universally depicted scenes in Christian art. There is perhaps not a Catholic church the world over which does not house one or the other image, and often both. But today's saint, Sebastian, follows close behind in terms of popularity and ubiquity. The iconic presentation of the wounded Sebastian shows his hands and arms bound to a post, his head tilted, and his almost naked body filled with arrows.

It is a powerfully evocative image. It suggests that the archers took their time. They were not rushed. They did not act in the heat of anger. Criminal psychologists have observed that killers only cover the faces of victims who they know. Otherwise, killers don't mind watching their victims suffer and die. It seems that with Sebastian there was no hooded executioner. No anonymous hangman. The men in Sebastian's firing squad must have gazed right into his eyes before they unleashed the tension in their bows. And when their arrows buried themselves in Sebastian's torso, the archers must have heard his low moans. Perhaps there was an element of recrimination in all of this. Perhaps it was personal.

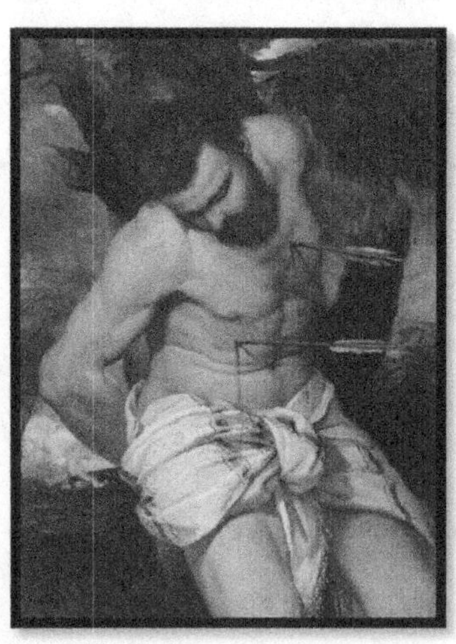

St. Sebastian
Frans Badens

Sebastian was a soldier in the higher echelons of the Roman army. After his conversion to Catholicism, he went to Rome, around the year 300, likely seeking martyrdom. We can imagine that his fellow soldiers understood his conversion as betrayal or disloyalty to the empire and that this explains the unique manner of the assassination attempt. But, in the end, the attempt was a failure. Saint Sebastian, a rugged soldier, survived the arrows, was nursed back to health by Saint Irene, and later earned the martyr's crown after being clubbed to death.

By the year 300 A.D., the Roman Emperors' attempts to eradicate Christianity were too little too late. Nobles, senators, slaves, cobblers, carpenters, men, women, foreigners, and natives had all converted. They were men and women of every class and occupation. By 300 A.D., Christians comprised a significant portion of people at every level of society, up and down and around every Roman road. When high-placed soldiers such as Saint Sebastian were willing to die for Christ, it was a sign there was no going back to Rome's pagan roots. All that was needed was a Christian

Emperor to solidify the change. That would come soon enough in the person of Constantine. Sebastian's heroic death was a harbinger of a world about to change. Saint Sebastian's martyrdom was so widely known that he was honored through the construction of a Church on the Appian Way just outside of Rome. The church is still visited by pilgrims today, along with the Christian catacombs beneath it. His legacy carries on!

Saint Sebastian, we ask your intercession to fortify all those who are weak in their faith. You gave heroic witness in leaving a high station to accept a near martyrdom and then returned to suffer and die once and for all. Give us the grace to face our enemies when our weak nature wants to run the other way.

January 21: Saint Agnes, Virgin and Martyr

c. 291–c. 304

Memorial; Liturgical Color: Red or White

Patron Saint of young girls, rape victims, and chastity

A child knows that God is a person who deserves to be loved

The names of only the earliest saints and martyrs are embedded in the Roman Canon, Eucharistic Prayer I. Saint Agnes is among those listed (Felicity, Perpetua, Agatha, Lucy, Agnes, Cecilia, Anastasia, etc.). Devotion to Agnes as both Virgin and Martyr is of ancient origin and is specifically mentioned by fourth-century writers, including Pope Damasus. A basilica was built as early as the reign of Constantine over the catacombs where Saint Agnes' relics were deposited. A later structure, with an ancient mosaic showing Saint Agnes, is still an active church on that exact same site today. The mobs of tourists and pilgrims who crowd the eternal city, and who shuffle through Piazza Navona today, may not realize that they are walking by the very site where Agnes was martyred. The beautiful Baroque Church of Saint Agnes on Piazza Navona reminds the discerning pilgrim that our saint met her death at that exact spot.

Agnes was of a tender age when she was killed. She was just a girl. Tradition says that she was beautiful and wanted to dedicate her virginity to the Lord, despite numerous suitors desirous of her beauty. She was killed, then, both for her faith and for her steadfastness in refusing to violate her vow of chastity. It was a double martyrdom, made all the sweeter because of her youth. With poetic license and rhetorical power, Saint Ambrose imagines Saint Agnes' final moments: "You could see fear in the eyes of the executioner, as if he were the one condemned; his right hand trembled; his face grew pale as he saw the girl's peril; while she had no fear for herself. One victim but a twin martyrdom to modesty and to religion. Agnes preserved her virginity and gained a martyr's crown."

When making solemn vows at his ordination, a man marries the Church so that he can make her fruitful. But a woman's religious vows make her a spouse of Christ Himself. A man marries the Church; a woman marries Christ. This beautiful bridal imagery speaks the human language of love and commitment. God is a person, not just a prime mover or a higher power. So He loves us like a person, and we love Him back like a person. Part of this love is jealousy. God is a jealous spouse. He wants total commitment from those who have dedicated their lives to Him. He demands total fidelity. In extreme cases, even to the point of death. Little Saint Agnes understood all of this with girlish simplicity united to a will of iron. Innocence alongside maturity. Chastity alongside toughness. Beauty holding hands with death.

Saint Agnes, help all young people commit themselves to Christ when young, giving Him the most fruitful years of their lives. Inspire them to say "Yes" to God and not just "No" to the world. Help all to see that although life is a gift, there are greater things than life, such as God in His glory.

January 22: Saint Vincent, Deacon and Martyr

Late Third Century–c. 304
Memorial; Liturgical Color: Red
Patron Saint of vintners, brickmakers, and sailors

A Deacon's bloody witness impresses the Christian world

There are a few famous saints who bear the name Vincent. Today's saint is the first Vincent. He was a deacon from the town of Zaragoza, Spain. Zaragoza hosts a famous shrine to Our Lady of the Pillar based on an appearance of the Virgin Mary there so ancient that it is more precisely described as a bilocation. Saint Vincent certainly knew of this devotion in his hometown. So although Saint Vincent is an early saint, he was from a city that, in 300 A.D., already boasted of a mature Christian tradition.

As with so many martyrs whose names are known to us, Vincent died in the persecution of Diocletian, the last gasps of a dying paganism. Vincent and his bishop were imprisoned around 303 and taken in chains to Valencia on Spain's Mediterranean coast. The bishop was exiled, but Vincent was subjected to such cruel and varied tortures that he died of his wounds. Tradition says that the faithful came to his cell during his sufferings seeking relics, even dipping cloths into his bloody wounds.

Although pious oral traditions led medieval authors to embroider some of the details of the Church's early saints and martyrs, the core facts of these narratives almost always have support. In Vincent's case, no less an authority than Saint Augustine gave homilies on Saint Vincent which have been preserved. In these, Augustine states that he has the official acts recounting Vincent's martyrdom right in front of him as he is speaking. That interesting anecdote, a kind of live shot of Augustine preaching, is a wonderful proof of how widespread devotion to Vincent was in the early Church, even far from where he died.

Ordained permanent deacons disappeared from the life of the church for many centuries, only to be reintroduced in the decades after the Second Vatican Council. Yet deacons' key roles in preaching, serving the poor, evangelizing, and acting as delegates of their bishops are clear from the Acts of the Apostles and Saint Paul's letters. As early as the second century after Christ, the three Orders constituting the Sacrament of Holy Orders were already clearly identified and theologically developed, especially in the letters of Saint Ignatius of Antioch. Ignatius saw each Order as participating, in a different way, in the one priesthood of the High Priest Jesus Christ.

It must be remembered that Vincent was a deacon and was imprisoned along with the bishop who ordained him. He must have understood the harmony and interdependence that God intended to exist among deacons, priests, and bishops. This emphasis on Sacramental Orders underlines the fact that, although early Christians may have experienced more astounding gifts of the Holy

Spirit than later Christians, it was still a living connection to an Apostle, not a personal charism, that authenticated and guaranteed one's participation in the true body of Christ. Gifts were personal and private. They came and went. They could not be verified or even shared. But each bishop was linked to an Apostolic See, and bishops publicly ordained priests and deacons to share the duty to teach, govern, and sanctify the baptized. There was nothing private about any of that.

Early Christianity was not a haphazard grouping of people who loved Jesus. It received a hierarchical structure from Christ Himself and immediately perpetuated, and built upon, Jewish forms of religious community life. The Church's hierarchical community life continues today. Saint Vincent undoubtedly saw his ordination as a form of service, not power. He was undoubtedly a man of great importance to his bishop. He likely gave generous witness to the Faith before he offered up his earthly life for a richer life beyond the grave.

Saint Vincent, help all deacons to know, love, and serve God with all their heart, soul, and mind. Few people are called to be tortured for the faith as you were, but suffering may come in more subtle ways. Help us to persevere in the face of all challenges so that we deepen our trust in God.

January 22: Day of Prayer for the Legal Protection of Unborn Children (U.S.A.)

Memorial; Liturgical Color: White or Violet

Abortion is a black eye on the handsome face of America

At 3:00 a.m. on March 13, 1964, a young woman parked her car next to her apartment building in Queens, New York. She got out and started walking toward the door when, in the darkness, she spotted someone in her path. She changed direction and ran toward a police call box. The man caught up and tackled her to the ground. He stabbed her in the back. She screamed for help. Lights blinked on; windows opened. She screamed repeatedly, "I'm dying! Help me!" The attack continued. Forty-five minutes later, a neighbor called the police. Officers arrived and identified the victim as twenty-eight-year-old Kitty Genovese. At least thirty-eight neighbors heard or witnessed the attack. Not one of them came to her aid. Only one called the police, belatedly.

The response to Kitty Genovese's murder was widely studied and became known as the "Genovese Syndrome" or the "Bystander Effect." As the number of bystanders to a crime or accident increases, the likelihood of anyone doing anything about it decreases. Because everyone thinks someone else is going to intervene, no one does anything. Ironically, if Kitty's attack had been witnessed by just one person, instead of thirty-eight, her chances of survival would have increased.

Moral outrage is stifled, duty is diminished, and the desire to blend in predominates in groups. Even if a group is witnessing something awful, many individuals keep quiet. January 22, 1973, marks the dark anniversary of the U.S. Supreme Court decisions, Roe vs. Wade and Doe vs. Bolton, which blew the moral lights out for the protection of the unborn in the United States. All right-thinking people have an obligation to name abortion for what it is, regardless of what others may say. A country is like a big group, and we tend to conform to group norms. But scientific and technological advances have erased all doubt about whether pre-born life is human life. It's a baby. When a woman is expecting, no one goes to a "fetus shower," they go to a "baby shower." It's not a potential human life. It's a human life with potential.

Dr. Bernard Nathanson, Jewish by blood and atheist by faith, was a Canadian American doctor who not only advocated for the legalization of abortion, but who also, with his own hands, aborted two of his own children. He is considered the "father" of the legalization of abortion in America, which culminated in the judicial decisions remembered today. One day in the mid-1970s, a doctor friend invited Nathanson to hold the ultrasound imaging paddle on a woman's belly as the doctor aborted her child. Nathanson was horrified at what was displayed on the ultrasound screen. The baby was vigorously flailing, trying to avoid the doctor's instruments, pushing against the sharp objects jabbing his body. And then the baby's mouth opened in a silent scream for help. Soon after, Dr. Nathanson gave up his lucrative abortion practice. And years later, after long and painful soul searching, Dr. Nathanson bowed his head to receive the waters of baptism in the Catholic Church, a real religion that forgives real sins.

Abortion corrupts all that it touches: family life, relationships between men and women, politicians, courts, doctors and nurses, and public life in general, which has become more hardened to the sufferings and vulnerabilities of those on the margins. But most of all, abortion has harmed every woman who has had one. There are psychological repercussions to the unnatural end of any pregnancy, but most especially when that end is violent, willful, and paid for by the one it harms. When the natural maternal instinct to nurture and protect is so violated, mom may never recover. The wound remains open. The healing is long and partial.

In this liturgical memorial, we commemorate an anniversary. So…Happy Anniversary, Abortion. You deceive, you divide, you destroy. You are darkness, and you are death. You are the bloody nose on the beautiful face of America. We pray that someday people will only speak about you in hushed tones, behind closed doors, whispering "abortion" like a dirty word. Happy Anniversary, Abortion; you are the pride in the devil's grin.

Heavenly Father and Mother Mary, today we storm heaven with our prayers, fasting, and almsgiving in the hope that all unborn children will be protected in law so that they can grow into the men and women you planned them to be.

January 23: Saint Marianne Cope, Virgin (U.S.A.)

1838–1918

Optional Memorial; Liturgical Color: White

Patron Saint of Hawai'i, lepers, outcasts, and sufferers of HIV/AIDS

She learned generosity at home and lived it her whole life

Today's saint was a model female Franciscan who emulated Saint Francis' heroic example of personally caring for the outcasts of all outcasts—lepers. Saints are not born, of course; they are made. And Saint Marianne Cope came from a specific time, place, and family. She could have developed her abundant talents in many directions and used them for many purposes, but she re-directed what God loaned her to serve Him, His Church, and mankind. The Church, the Franciscans, and Hawai'i were the arenas in which this elite spiritual athlete exercised her skills. She was asked for much and gave even more. She became a great woman.

Marianne Cope was born in Germany and was brought to New York state by her parents when she was still a baby. She was the oldest of ten children. Her parents lived, struggled, and worked for their kids. She saw generosity in action at home every day. She quit school after eighth grade to work in a factory to financially support her ailing father, her mother, and her many siblings. The challenges inherent to immigration, a new culture, illness, a large family, and poverty turned Marianne into a serious, mature woman when she was just a teen.

Marianne fulfilled her long-delayed desire to enter religious life in 1862. Once professed, she moved quickly into leadership positions. She taught in German-speaking Catholic grade schools, became a school principal, and was elected by her fellow Franciscans to positions of governance in her Order. She opened the first hospitals in her region of Central New York, dedicating herself and her Order to the time-honored religious vocation of caring for the sick, regardless of their ability to pay for medical services. She was eventually elected Superior General. In her early forties, she was already a woman of wide experience: serious, administratively gifted, spiritually grounded, and of great human virtues. But this was all mere preparation. She now began the second great act of her drama. She went to Hawai'i.

In 1883 she received a letter from the Bishop of Honolulu begging her, as Superior General, to send sisters to care for lepers in Hawai'i. He had written to various other religious Orders without success. Sister Marianne was elated. She responded like the prophet Isaiah, saying, "Here am I; send me!" (Is 6:8). She not only sent six sisters, she sent herself! She planned to one day return to New York but never did. For the next thirty-five years, Sister Marianne Cope became a type of recluse on remote Hawai'i, giving herself completely to the will of God.

Sister Marianne and her fellow Franciscans managed one hospital, founded another, opened a home for the daughters of lepers, and, after a few years of proving themselves, opened a home for women and girls on the virtually inaccessible island of Molokai. Here her life coincided with the final months of Saint Damien de Veuster. Sister Marianne nursed the future saint in his dying days, assuring him that she and her sisters would continue his work among the lepers. After Father Damien died, the Franciscans, in addition to caring for the leprous girls, now cared for the boys too. A male Congregation eventually relieved them of this apostolate.

Sister Marianne Cope lived the last thirty years of her life on Molokai until her death in 1918. She was beatified by Pope Benedict XVI in 2005 and canonized by him in 2012. She loved the Holy Eucharist, the Virgin Mary, and the Church. And because she loved God first, she loved those whom God loves, her brothers and sisters in Christ. She sacrificed for them, left home and family for them, put her health at risk for them, and became a saint through them.

Saint Marianne Cope, help us to be as generous as you were in serving those on the margins, those who need our help, and those who have no one else to assist them. You were a model Franciscan in dying to self. Help us to likewise die so that we might likewise live.

January 24: Saint Francis de Sales, Bishop

1567–1622

Memorial; Liturgical Color: White

Patron Saint of writers and journalists

A talented gentleman of sterling character embodies holiness

It is almost an act of rudeness to limit the life of today's saint to a page or two. Saint Francis de Sales was a religious celebrity in his own day and age. He was an erudite, humble, tough, and zealous priest and bishop. He was holy and known to be holy by everyone, especially those closest to him. He mingled easily with princes, kings, and popes, who enjoyed his charming and educated company. He incessantly crisscrossed his diocese on foot and horseback, destroying his own health, to visit the poor and humble faithful who were drawn to him as much as the high born. He embodied to the fullest that extraordinary pastoral and intellectual productivity, characteristic of the greatest saints, which makes one wonder if he ever rested a single minute or slept a single night.

Saint Francis de Sales was born and lived most of his life in what is today Southeast France. His father ensured that he received an excellent education from a young age, and his son excelled in every subject. His intellectual gifts, holiness, and engaging personality made him, almost inevitably, an ideal candidate for the priesthood and eventually the episcopacy. He was duly appointed the Bishop of Geneva, a generation after John Calvin, a former future priest, had turned that deeply Catholic city into the Protestant Rome. Saint Francis was Bishop of Geneva primarily in name, not fact.

In carrying out his ministry, Francis' weapon of choice was the pen. His apologetic and spiritual works brought back to the faith tens of thousands of former Catholics after they had dabbled in Calvinism. Saint Francis's works were so profound and creative, and his love of God so straightforward and understandable, that he would be declared a Doctor of the Church in 1877. In his most well-known book, *Introduction to the Devout Life*, he addressed himself to "people who live in towns, within families, or at court." His sage spiritual advice encouraged the faithful to seek perfection in the mechanic's shop, the soldier's regiment, or on the wharf. God's will was to be found everywhere, not just in monasteries and convents.

Many arduous pastoral trips through the mountains of his native region eventually wore him out. Saint Francis never insisted on preferential treatment despite his status. He slept, ate, and traveled as a common man would. When he lay dying, mute after a terrible stroke, a nun asked him if he had any final words of wisdom to impart. He asked for some paper and wrote three words on it: "Humility, Humility, Humility." Saint Francis is buried in a beautiful bronze sepulchre displaying his likeness in the Visitation Basilica and Convent in Annecy, France.

Saint Francis de Sales, we ask your intercession to aid us in leading a balanced life of study, prayer, virtue, and service. You were a model bishop who never expected special privilege. Help all those who teach the faith to convey doctrine with the same force, clarity, and depth that you did.

January 25: The Conversion of Saint Paul

First Century

Feast; Liturgical Color: White

Patron Saint of missionaries, evangelists, and writers

One man can change the world

In the long history of the Church, no conversion has been more consequential than Saint Paul's. Paul had not been ambivalent toward the Church before he converted. He had actively persecuted it, even throwing rocks at the head of Saint Stephen, in all likelihood. But he changed, or God changed him, on one particular night. And on that night, Christianity changed too. And when the course of Christianity changed, the world changed. It is difficult to overemphasize the import of Saint Paul's conversion.

One way to think about the significance of an event, whether big or small, is to consider what things would have been like if the event had never occurred. This is the premise behind the movie "It's a Wonderful Life." You compare actual life with a hypothetical "what if" alternative scenario. What if Saint Paul had remained a zealous Jew? What if he had never converted? Never wrote one letter? Never travelled the high seas on missionary voyages? It can safely be assumed that the world itself, not just the Church, would look different than it does today. Perhaps Christianity would have remained confined to Palestine for many more centuries before breaking out into wider Europe. Maybe Christianity would have taken a right turn instead of a left, and all of China and India would be as culturally Catholic as Europe is today. It's impossible to say. But the global scale of the effects of Paul's ministry speak to the significance of his conversion.

Some conversions are dramatic, some boring. Some are instantaneous, some gradual. Augustine heard a boy in a garden repeating, "Take and Read," and knew the time had come. Saint Francis heard Christ say from the cross, "Rebuild My Church," and responded with his life. Dr. Bernard Nathanson, the father of abortion in the United States, repudiated and repented of his life's work and searched for a real Church to forgive his real sins. He ultimately bowed his head to receive the waters of baptism.

The details of Paul's conversion are well known. He was, perhaps, thrown from his horse on the road to Damascus (except that Acts makes no mention of a horse). Maybe he just fell down while walking. While stunned on the ground, Paul heard the voice of Jesus ask: "Why are you persecuting me?"—not "Why are you persecuting my followers." Jesus and the Church are clearly one. To persecute the Church is to persecute Christ. Jesus is the head, and the Church is His body. Paul did not convert to loving Jesus while saying that the Church was just an accidental human construct that blocked him from the Lord. No, of course not! He believed what right-minded Catholics have believed for centuries and still believe today. To love Jesus is to love the Church, and vice versa. It is impossible to love the Lord while disregarding the historical reality of how the Lord is communicated to us. The Church is not just a vehicle to carry God's revelation. The Church is as much a part of God's revelation as Scripture.

Paul's conversion teaches us that when Jesus comes to us, He doesn't come alone. He comes with His angels, saints, priests, and bishops. He comes with Mary, the sacraments, doctrine, and devotions. He comes with the Church, because He and the Church are one. And when we go to the Lord, we don't go alone either. We go as members of a Church into whose mystical body we were baptized. Thus Saint Paul heard from God Himself, and thus we believe today.

Saint Paul, we ask your openness to conversion when we hear the Lord speak to us as He spoke to you. Assist us in responding with great faith to every invitation we receive to love the Lord more fully, to know Him more deeply, and to spread His word more broadly to those who need it.

The Conversion on the Way to Damascus
Michelangelo Merisi da Caravaggio

January 26: Saints Timothy and Titus, Bishops

First Century

Memorial; Liturgical Color: White

Patron Saints of stomach disorders

Saint Paul could not do it alone

Today's saints were two bishops from the apostolic period of the Church, those decades immediately following the death and resurrection of Our Lord. In this grace-filled time, the Apostles and Saint Paul were carving the first deep furrows into the pagan soil they traveled, planting in the earth the rich seeds of Christian faith which succeeding bishops would later water, tend, and harvest.

Little is certainly known about today's saints apart from references to them in the Acts of the Apostles and in the Epistles of Saint Paul. But these numerous references are enough. The generations of theologians, bishops, martyrs, and saints who lived in the post-apostolic period give universal and consistent witness to the veracity of Paul's letters and the events they recount. There are theological, more than historical, lessons to be taken from the lives and ministry of today's saints.

Saints Timothy and Titus were apostles of an Apostle. They shared in the ministry of Saint Paul, who had a direct connection to Christ through a miraculous occurrence on the road to Damascus, a feast commemorated, not coincidentally, the day prior to today's memorial. Timothy, Titus, and many others, known and unknown, carried out on a local level a priestly ministry which Paul engaged in on a more regional level. It was Saint Paul's practice, and probably that of the other surviving Apostles, to appoint assistants wherever they went who acted with the authority of the Apostle who appointed them. These assistants were variously called priests or bishops, terms that were often interchangeable. Deacons, of course, shared in the priestly ministry too, but more as assistants to bishops.

A direct connection to an Apostle, either through his personal ministry or through a group or delegate he appointed (through an ordination rite), was fundamental to establishing a church. Accredited leaders were needed. This is a constant theme in the writings of Saint Paul. No Apostle—no Church. The body could not be separated from the head and still survive. In other words, the faithful proclamation of the Gospel always—always—occurred contemporaneously with the foundation of a solidly structured local Church. The modern tendency to emphasize the internal, personal, and spiritual message of Christ over the external, public, hierarchical Church which carries His message is a dichotomy unknown to early Christianity. For early Christians and faithful Christians still today, the Church carries a message and is itself a message. The content of the Gospel and the form of the Gospel community go hand in hand. The constant, amoeba-like splitting of Protestant communities attests to the inevitable divisions which result when the Church and its message are separated.

A later tradition holds that Saint Timothy was the first Bishop of Ephesus, in modern-day Turkey. Equally ancient traditions state that Saint John the Evangelist retreated to Ephesus before dying on the island of Patmos, and that Mary followed John to Ephesus, living in a house above the town. It is possible, then, that Saint Timothy drank from the deepest wells of the Christian tradition. Sitting around the warm glow of a fire at night, he may have heard about the life of Christ from the very lips of the most important witnesses—Mary and John. We can imagine that Timothy heard about many of the unwritten events of Christ's life from Saint John. It is this same John who ends his Gospel by writing that "there are also many other things that Jesus did; if every one of them were written down, I suppose that the world itself could not contain the books that would be written" (Jn 21:25). Timothy and Titus were bearers of the very oldest Christian traditions.

Saints Timothy and Titus, through your lives dedicated to the missions, you helped lay the foundations of Christianity, and carried on the priestly ministry of Jesus by preaching, teaching, and governing His flock. Help us to be as bold now as you were then.

January 27: Saint Angela Merici, Virgin

1474–1540

Optional Memorial; Liturgical Color: White

Patron Saint of disabled and physically challenged people and illnesses

A holy woman tries to change the world one girl at a time

Although not common, some older images and statues of Saint Francis of Assisi show him balancing three orbs on his shoulders. They appear to be globes, heavenly realms, or the earth, the moon, and the sun. But the three orbs actually represent the three orders in the Franciscan family: the first order for men, the second order for women, and the third order for the laity who desire to live by the Franciscan Rule. Today's saint, Angela Merici, was a Third Order Franciscan, a lay woman who followed a strict rule of Franciscan life outside of a convent.

Angela's holiness, mystical experiences, and leadership skills ultimately led her beyond her Franciscan commitment to found her own community of "virgins in the world" dedicated to the education of vulnerable girls or, in modern parlance, at-risk youths. She placed the community under the patronage of Saint Ursula. The community, after Angela's death, was formally recognized as the Ursulines and gained such renown for their schools that they came to be known as the female Jesuits.

Saint Angela saw the risk that uneducated girls in her native region of Northern Italy would end up being abused sexually or financially and sought to counter these possible outcomes through education. She gathered a like-minded group of virgins around her into a "company," a military word also used by Saint Ignatius in founding his "Company of Jesus" around the same time. Saint Angela organized her city into districts which reported to "colonels" who oversaw the education and general welfare of the poor girls under their care. Saint Angela's cooperators did not understand their dedicated virginity as a failure to find a husband or a rejection of religious life in a convent. They emulated the early Christian orders of virgins as spouses of Christ who served the children of their Beloved in the world.

Living in the first part of the sixteenth century, Saint Angela was far ahead of her time. Teaching orders of nuns became normative in the Church in later centuries, staffing Catholic schools throughout the world. But nuns did not always do this. This practice had to start with someone, and that someone was today's saint. Bonds of faith, love of God, and a common purpose knitted her followers together into a religious family that served the spiritual and physical welfare of those who no one else cared about. Women make a house a home, and Saint Angela sought to change society one woman at a time by infusing every home with Christian virtue emanating from the heart of the woman who ran it. She trained future wives, mothers, and educators in their youth, when they were still able to be formed.

The Papal Bull of Pope Paul III in 1544, which canonically recognized her community, stated of Saint Angela Merici: "She had such a thirst and hunger for the salvation and good of her neighbor that she was disposed and most ready to give not one, but a thousand lives, if she had had so many, for the salvation even of the least…with maternal love, she embraced all creatures...Her words...were spoken with such unheard of effectiveness that everyone felt compelled to say: 'Here is God.'"

Saint Angela Merici, infuse in our hearts that same love for which you left worldly joys to seek out the vulnerable and the forgotten. Help us to educate the ignorant and to share with the less fortunate, not only for their spiritual and material benefit but for our everlasting salvation.

January 28: Saint Thomas Aquinas, Priest and Doctor

1225–1274

Memorial; Liturgical Color: White

Patron Saint of universities and students

A theological Grand Master, he positioned every piece exquisitely on the chessboard

The silhouette of Saint Thomas Aquinas hovers like a giant on the highest summit of human thought, casting so wide and deep a shadow over the landscape that all subsequent thinkers labor on the shady slopes below him. It is fair to say that Thomism, the thinking method and intellectual conclusions of Saint Thomas, has been the

Catholic Church's standard theology since he lived in the thirteenth century.

Saint Thomas understood that all thinking about God is done from inside original sin and within the parameters of human intellectual capacity. The uncreated, timeless, mysterious God, then, is by definition incomprehensible to creatures trapped in time, space, matter, sin, distraction, and confusion. God is outside of the universe, rather than being just one important ingredient in the recipe of reality. This essential "otherness" of God means that His presence is not completely accessible to the senses. It is not just a question of seeing farther, understanding more deeply, hearing more acutely, or feeling more intensely. Twenty senses instead of five would still not be enough to capture God, because He transcends all other forms of being known to us. In the 1950s, a Russian cosmonaut looked out over space from his orbit miles above the earth and declared "I have found no God." He was looking for something that wasn't there and answering a question that was poorly posed.

Sometimes God is described as the highest being in an immense hierarchy of beings. From this perspective, the tiniest specks of organic or inorganic life, up and onward through plant and animal life, mankind, the planets and the solar system itself, are all beneath and owe their creation to the super being of God Himself. In this "ladder-of-existence" understanding, every being is a rung leading to higher and higher rungs at the top of which stands God.

Such an understanding of God is inaccurate, Aquinas would hold. God is not the highest of all beings but Being itself. Every person at one time did not exist. Creation itself, including mankind, is created, meaning at some point it was not. But God cannot not be. For Saint Thomas, God's essential action is to exist. It is intrinsic to His nature as God. God, then, is not something in the air but the air itself. He is not the biggest whale in the ocean. He is the water. This means that there is no strict need to provide scientific evidence for God, because even asking the question presumes the reality all around us. Science, for example, can explain the chemical composition of ink, but it has nothing to say about the meaning of words printed in ink. Science clearly has limits.

ST. THOMAS AQUINAS, O.P.

January 28

"Grant me, O Lord my God, a mind to know you,
a heart to seek you, wisdom to find you,
conduct pleasing to you,
faithful perseverance in waiting for you,
and a hope of finally embracing you.
Amen."

Thomism's understanding of God as non-contingent being, which makes all dependent existence possible, is intellectually sophisticated and also deeply attractive. This understanding of God meshes nicely with an appreciation for the natural beauty of the earth, love of art, and charity for our fellow man, while also allowing space for God to reveal Himself more fully, and gratuitously, in the person of His Son Jesus Christ. Importantly, it also avoids confusing God's creation with God Himself.

Saint Thomas's encyclopedic knowledge and massive erudition existed harmoniously with a humble nature and a simple, traditional Catholic piety. He was a well-balanced man and a dedicated Dominican priest. This synthesis of childlike wonder and deep inquiry marked his life. After having a mystical vision of Jesus Christ on the cross while praying after Mass one day, Saint Thomas abandoned any further writing. He died on his way to the Second Council of Lyon in 1274, not yet fifty years old. He is buried in Toulouse, France, retaining his status as the Church's most eminent theologian.

Saint Thomas, your life of the mind co-existed with a deep piety. Your writings defend the faith of those who have neither the time nor the gift for higher study. Help all those who teach in the Church to follow your example of humble and faithful inquiry into the highest truths.

January 31: Saint John Bosco, Priest

1815–1888

Memorial; Liturgical Color: White

Patron Saint of editors, publishers, schoolchildren, and juvenile delinquents

His fatherly heart radiated the warm love of God

Some saints attract the faithful by the raw power of their minds and the sheer force of their arguments. Think of Saint Thomas Aquinas or Saint Augustine. Other saints write so eloquently, with such grace and sweetness, that their words draw people to God like bees to honey. Think of Saint John Henry Newman or Saint Francis de Sales. Still other saints say and write almost nothing, but lead lives of such generous and sacrificial witness that their holiness is obvious. Think of Saint Francis of Assisi or Saint Teresa of Calcutta. Today's saint was not a first-class thinker, eloquent writer, bloody martyr, or path-breaking Church reformer. Yet his abundant gifts drew people to God in their own unique way.

Saint John Bosco was, to put it in the simplest terms, a winner. His heart was like a furnace radiating immense warmth, fraternal concern, and affectionate love of God. His personality seemed to operate like a powerful magnet that pulled everyone closer and closer in toward his overflowing, priestly, and fatherly love. His country-boy simplicity, street smarts, genuine concern for the poor, and love of God, Mary, and the Church made him irresistible. Don Bosco ('Don' being a title of honor for priests, teachers, etc.) had charm. What he asked for, he received. From everyone. He built, during his own lifetime, an international empire of charity and education so massive and so successful that it is impossible to explain his accomplishments in merely human terms.

Like many great saints, Don Bosco's external, observable charisms were not the whole story. Behind his engaging personality was a will like a rod of iron. He exercised strict self-discipline and firmness of purpose in driving toward his goals. His gift of self, or self-dedication, was remarkable. Morning, noon, and night. Weekday or weekend. Rain or shine. He was always there. Unhurried. Available. Ready to talk. His life was one big generous act from beginning to end.

Saint John grew up dirt poor in the country working as a shepherd. His father died when he was an infant. After studies and priestly ordination, he went to the big city, Turin, and saw first-hand how the urban poor lived. It changed his life. He began a ministry to poor boys which was not particularly innovative. He said Mass, heard confessions, taught the Gospel, went on walks, cooked meals, and taught practical skills like book binding. There was no secret to Don Bosco's success. But no one else was doing it, and no one else did it so well. Followers flocked to assist him, and he founded the Salesians, a Congregation named after his own hero, Saint Francis de Sales. The Salesian empire of charity and education spread around the globe. By the time of its founder's death in 1888, the Salesians had 250 houses the world over, caring for 130,000 children. Their work continues today.

ST. JOHN BOSCO

January 31

"Fly from bad companions as from the bite of a poisonous snake."

Don Bosco was not concerned with the remote causes of poverty. He did not challenge class structures or economic systems. He saw what was in front of him and went "straight to the poor," as he put it. He did his work from the inside out. It was for others to figure out long-term solutions, not for him. Don Bosco did not know what rest was and wore himself out by being all things to all men. His reputation for holiness endured well beyond his death. A young priest who had met him in Northern Italy in 1883, Father Achille Ratti, later became Pope Pius XI. On Easter Sunday 1934, this same pope canonized the great Don Bosco whom he had known so many years before.

Saint John Bosco, you dedicated your life to the education and care of poor youth. Aid us in reaching out to those who need our assistance today, not tomorrow, and here, not somewhere else. Through your intercession, may we carry out a fraction of the good that you achieved in your life.

FEBRUARY

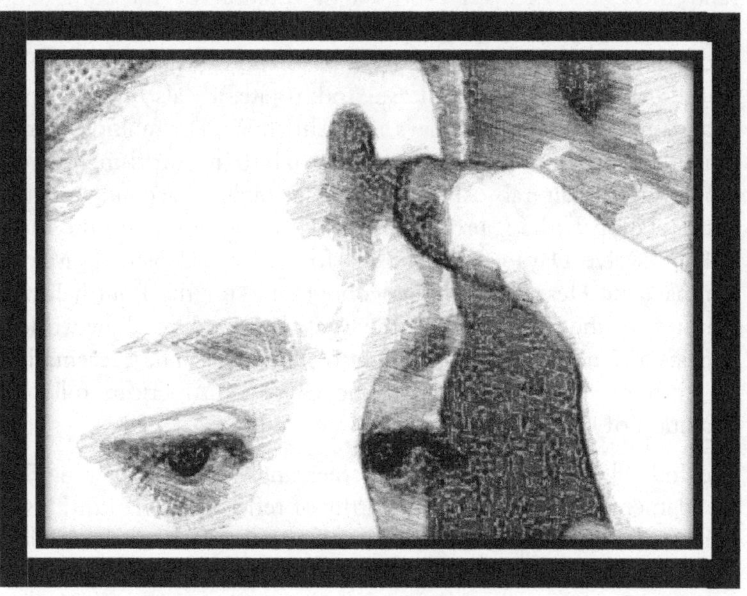

"…and to dust you shall return."

February 2: The Presentation of the Lord

Feast; Liturgical Color: White

God goes to Church

The various names, meanings, and traditions overlapping in today's Feast churn like the crystals in a kaleidoscope, revealing one image and then another with every slight rotation of the tube. The Presentation of the Lord in the Temple is, rotate, also the Purification of Mary. But, rotate, it's also known as the "Meeting of the Lord" in the Christian East. And, rotate, it's also the Feast of Candlemas, marking forty days after Christmas. The multiple names and meanings of today's Feast have given birth to surprisingly broad and varied cultural expressions. The biblical account of the Presentation is the source for the "two turtle doves" in the carol "The Twelve Days of Christmas," for the sword piercing Mary's Immaculate Heart in Catholic iconography, for the Fourth Joyful Mystery of the rosary, and for the Canticle prayed by all the world's priests and nuns every single night of their lives. The Presentation is even the remote source of the frivolous American folkloric tradition of Groundhog Day.

Behind all of these names and meanings are, however, a few fundamental theological facts worthy of reflection. The Lord Jesus Christ, forty days after His birth, in keeping with both the biblical significance of the number forty and with Jewish custom, was presented in the temple in Jerusalem by His parents, Mary and Joseph. Saint Luke's Gospel recounts the story. After the Presentation, Jesus was to enter the temple again as a boy and later as an adult. He would even refer to His own body as a temple which He would raise up in three days. Jesus's life was a continual self-gift to God the Father from the very beginning to the very end. His parents did not carry their infant Son to a holy mountain, a sacred spring, or a magical forest. It was in His temple that the God of Israel was most present, so they brought their Son to God Himself, not just to a reflection of Him in nature.

The extraordinarily beautiful temple in Jerusalem, the building where Jesus was presented by His parents, was burned to ashes by a powerful Roman army under the future Emperor Titus in 70 A.D.

It was never rebuilt. A tourist in Rome can, even today, gaze up at the marble depictions of the sack of the Jerusalem Temple carved on the inside vaults of the Arch of Titus in the Roman Forum. Christianity has never had just one sacred place equivalent to the Jewish Temple or the Muslims' Kaaba in Mecca. Christianity is historical, yes, but it has a global reach rising above any one culture or region.

Christ is destined for all cultures and all times. Every Catholic church with the Blessed Sacrament is a Holy of Holies, which fully expresses the deepest mysteries of our faith. There is no strict need to go on pilgrimage to Rome or to Jerusalem once in your life. But you do have to go on pilgrimage to your local parish once a week for Mass. Every Catholic church in every place, not just one building in one place, encompasses and transmits the entirety of our faith. God's hand must have been involved in the headship of the Church migrating from Jerusalem to Rome in the first century. Our Pope does not live in the historical cradle of the faith he represents, because Saint Peter saw no need to remain in Jerusalem in order to be faithful to his Master. The Church is where Christ is, Christ is in the Holy Eucharist, and the Holy Eucharist is everywhere.

We go to church, as the Jews went to their one temple or to their many synagogues, because God is more God in a church. And when we experience the true God, we experience our true selves. That is, we are more us when God is more God. God is interpreted according to the mode of the interpreter when He is sought in a glowing sunset, a rushing waterfall, or a stunning mountain. In nature, God is whoever the seeker wants Him to be. In a church, however, God is protected from misinterpretation. He is surrounded and protected by His priests, saints, sacraments, music, art, and worship. In a church, God is fully clothed, equipped, and armored. He is less likely to be misunderstood. So we go to find Him there, to dedicate ourselves to Him there, and to receive Him there in His Body and in His Blood.

Lord Jesus, as an infant You were brought to the temple by Your parents out of religious duty. Help all parents to take their duties to God seriously, to inculcate their faith in the next generation by their words and actions, so that the faith will be handed on where the faith is first learned—in the family and in the home.

February 3: Saint Blaise, Bishop and Martyr

c. Early Fourth Century

Optional Memorial; Liturgical Color: Red

Patron Saint of wool combers and sufferers of throat diseases

The memory of an obscure bishop-martyr endures

A secularist does not evaluate religion on its own terms but on its practical benefits. Is a religion true? It doesn't matter. But if you can prove that empty stomachs are now full, that malarial fevers are cooled, and that formerly dusty roads are now paved due to religion, then religion is indeed useful and good, all truth claims aside. Religion's role in physical healing would be another proof of its great good, if not its truth. For all the incontestable progress of medicine, cancers still spread, tumors still grow, and infections still poison. Even the most modern of moderns, in a state of total vulnerability, understands in his deepest of deeps that physical healings surge from sources other than modern science. PhDs wash in the River Ganges, rocket scientists lower their bodies into the cool baths of Lourdes, and surgeons spread sacred oil on their skin hoping against hope for a cure that has eluded medicine.

The memory of Saint Blaise, a man of obscure origins, stands behind one of the most enduring healing traditions in all of Christendom. In the holy name of Blaise, two candles are crossed, X-shaped, and pressed against the neck to ward off and cure diseases of the throat. Oils and relics, candles and flames, bread and wine, words and blessings. God's face does not appear in the ash cloud rising from a volcanic eruption or in a golden pile at the end of a rainbow. The Christian believes that God's salvation and healing power come through His Holy Mother, through His saints, and through the creation He molded in His own hands.

A believer doesn't believe in belief, any more than a soldier loves patriotism. A soldier loves his country, and a believer loves God. And because the believer loves God, he loves a someone, not a something, and waits in line and shuffles forward, step by step, to the priest holding those X-shaped candles on today's feast. Because it is usually winter, the believer adjusts his jacket collar, feels the milky wax candle against his tender throat, closes his eyes, and prays that the cough disappear, that his voice remain strong, or that the faintest lump turn out to be nothing at all. Saint Blaise is primarily a "Northern" saint invoked to remedy mostly cold-climate ills.

Details of Saint Blaise's life are difficult to verify. Some traditions, dating from centuries after he lived, state that he was a bishop in Armenia, east of modern-day Turkey. His reputation for holiness drew people to him in search of a cure for their infirmities. It is said that Blaise was tortured and murdered in an anti-Christian persecution. Every saint, no matter how remote his life or obscure his story, casts some light on the truths of our faith. The life of Saint Blaise and the tradition of throat healing that still surrounds him tell us that holy lives have power. His life tells us that holy people intercede for less holy people, and that the less powerful, the less wise, and the less good depend on the strong, the intelligent, and the virtuous in order to leave their state of dependence, ignorance, and sin.

In the same way that salvation is mediated, healing is as well. Whether through the skilled hands of a surgeon, the chemicals of a drug, or the intercession of a saint, healing comes. The many channels branch out from the one source who is God. We, the faithful, when fragile and afraid, patiently sit in the doctor's office for our name to be called, wait at the pharmacy counter for the prescription to be filled, or line up in church for the candles to rest softly on our clavicles. Healing is on offer, we are ripe to be cured, and any sacred intervention is welcome, no matter whence it comes.

Saint Blaise, many centuries ago you suffered for the same faith we now share with you. May we be ever united to you in our common Church, and may we be healed of all infirmities of the throat through your heavenly intercession.

February 3: Saint Ansgar, Bishop

801–865

Optional Memorial; Liturgical Color: White

Patron Saint of Scandinavia, Denmark, and Sweden

He sowed the frozen turf of the North, though little bloomed

Today's saint walked the forests of Northern Europe during that stretch of history later known, prejudicially, as the "Dark Ages." He lived three hundred years after the fall of Rome and yet three hundred years before the soaring gothic spires of the High Middle Ages pierced the blue sky. "Ansgar" is a grunt or a mere sound to modern ears. It seems fit for a remote, cold, and brutal age. It is difficult to imagine a child running into the warm embrace of a sunny Ansgar. But the real Saint Ansgar broke bread with Northern Vikings and rough warriors of the forest with names just like his own: Horik, Drogo, Gudmund, and Vedast. Ansgar was one of them, with one big difference—he was a Catholic.

The one thing, a very big thing, that links such long-ago saints, priests, and bishops to us moderns is the Catholic faith. We share the exact same faith as Saint Ansgar! If Saint Ansgar were to step out of the pages of a book today, in his bear fur pelt and deerskin boots, and walk through the doors of a twenty-first-century Catholic church, he would be at home. His eyes would search for the burning flame of the sanctuary lamp, and upon spotting it, he would know. He would bend his knee before a tabernacle housing the Blessed Sacrament, just as he did thousands of times in the past. He would walk past statues of Mary and the saints and know their stories. He would hear the same Gospel, make the same sign of the cross, and feel the same drops of blessed water on his forehead. Nothing would be unusual. Our faith unites what time and culture divide. The Church is the world's only multicultural, transnational, timeless family. There is nothing else like Her.

Saint Ansgar left his native region in Northern France, after receiving a good Christian education, to become an apostle monk to Northern Germany. He was named by the Pope as Archbishop of Hamburg and, from that post, organized the first systematic evangelization of Scandinavia. These regions were far, far away from the more developed civilizations of Italy, Spain, and France.

Yet Saint Ansgar and his helpers traveled that far, and risked that much, to plant the Catholic faith in the frozen ground of what is today Denmark, Norway, and Sweden.

Yet nearly all the seeds of faith that Saint Ansgar planted were to die in the ground shortly after his own death. Sadly, his missionary efforts produced no long-lasting fruit. The age of the Vikings dawned, and it would be two centuries before Christianity would again flourish and spread across the northern arc of Europe. Yet even that second evangelization would come to a bitter end! In the sixteenth century, Scandinavia abandoned Catholicism for its shadow under the influence of Father Luther and his followers.

What a lesson to be learned! As Saint Paul wrote, one plants, one waters, and God gives the growth: "The one who plants and the one who waters have a common purpose, and each will receive wages according to the labor of each" (1 Co 3:8). Saint Ansgar carried out God's will. He labored for the Lord and for the faith. What happened after that was up to God in His providence. Carrying out God's will should be enough for us, as it was for our saint today. We must plant and till, even though harvest time may never come.

Saint Ansgar, you persevered in difficult times to bring the faith to a pagan land. You saw success and then failure, glory and then disappointment. Your work did not outlast you but pleased God nonetheless. May we see our work as our duty, even when the fruit of our labor is harvested by someone else, or not at all.

February 5: Saint Agatha, Virgin and Martyr

c. Third Century

Memorial; Liturgical Color: Red

(When Lenten Weekday, Optional Memorial; Violet)

Patron Saint of Sicily, breast cancer, rape victims, and bellfounders

Of all the men drawn to her, she desired only one

Pope Saint Gregory the Great reigned as the Supreme Pontiff of the Church from 590–604. His family loved Sicily and had property there, so the young Gregory was familiar with that beautiful island's saints and traditions. When he became Pope, Saint Gregory inserted the names of two of Sicily's most revered martyrs, Agatha and Lucy, into the heart of the Mass, the Roman Canon. Saint Gregory even placed these two Sicilians just before the city of Rome's own two female martyrs, Agnes and Cecilia, who had been part of the Roman Canon for many centuries prior. It was this papal decision that has preserved Saint Agatha's memory more effectively than anything else. Liturgy is inherently conservative and protects the Church's oldest memories. So on the lips of thousands of priests every day are the names of some of the Church's most revered female martyrs: "Felicity, Perpetua, Agatha, Lucy, Agnes, Cecilia, Anastasia, and all the saints."

Not much is known for certain about the life and death of Saint Agatha, but long tradition supplies what primary documents lack. Pope Damasus (366–384) may have composed a poem in her honor, indicating how widespread her reputation was by that early date. Agatha was from a well-off family in Roman Sicily, probably in the third century. After dedicating her life to Christ, her beauty drew powerful men to her like a magnet. But she refused all suitors in favor of the Lord. Perhaps during the persecution of the Emperor Decius around 250, she was arrested, interrogated, tortured, and martyred. She refused to renounce her faith or to give in to the powerful men who desired her. An ancient homily relates: "A true virgin, she wore the glow of a pure conscience and the crimson of the lamb's blood for her cosmetics."

It is also the constant tradition that her torture included sexual mutilation. Saint Lucy is shown in art with her eyeballs on a platter. Saint Agatha is normally shown holding a plate on which rest her own breasts, as they were cut off by her pagan tormentors before her execution. This peculiar image is, in fact, carved into the entrance of Rome's sixth-century church of Saint Agatha, a church re-dedicated by Pope Saint Gregory himself so long ago.

Men commit most of the physical violence in the world. And when their victims are women, that violence can be particularly vicious because their victims are so defenseless. The stories of the early male martyrs of the Church relate tales of extreme torture by their Roman captors. But the stories of the women martyrs often relate something more—sexual humiliation. Few male martyrs

ST. AGATHA

February 5

"Behold the bright festal day of the glorious martyr
and virgin Agatha, when Christ took her to himself,
and a double crown wreathed her brow.
Though noble by birth, and blessed with beauty,
her grandest riches were her deeds and her faith."

– From an ancient poem to Saint Agatha

suffered similar indignities. Saint Agatha and others were not only physically tough to endure the pain they did but also mentally and spiritually powerful to have resisted, to the death, the public embarrassment and degradation particular to them as women. They were the strong ones. Their male captors looked weak.

It was Christianity's exaltation of women, children, slaves, prisoners, the old, the sick, the foreigner, and the outcast that caused the vast leaven of the Church to slowly rise in the Mediterranean world. The Church did not create a victim class who complained about a privileged class. The Church preached the dignity of persons. The Church did not even preach equality of individuals or teach that governments must enact laws protecting the unprotected. That is all so modern. The Church spoke in theological language and taught that every man, woman, and child was made in God's image and likeness and so deserved respect. It taught that Jesus Christ died on the Cross for every person. The Church gave, and gives, total answers to total questions, and those answers were, and are, compelling. The Feast of St. Agatha is still massively celebrated on February 5 in Catania, Sicily. Hundreds of thousands of faithful process through the streets in honor of that island's patron saint. The ancient traditions carry on.

Saint Agatha, you were a virgin espoused to Christ Himself, a bride of the Lord who preserved herself for Him alone. Your vow to love God above all else hardened you to endure temptation, torture, and degradation. May we be as resolute as you when any type of persecution, however mild, seeks us out.

February 6: Saint Paul Miki and Companions, Martyrs

St. Paul Miki: c. 1562–1597; Late Sixteenth Century
Memorial; Liturgical Color: Red
(When Lenten Weekday, Optional Memorial; Violet)
Patron Saints of Japan

Native Japanese die to gain the pearl of great price

The words of the American poet John Greenleaf Whittier capture the pathos of today's memorial: "For of all sad words of tongue or pen, The saddest are these: 'It might have been!'" The swift rise, and sudden fall, of Catholicism in Japan is one of the great "might-have-beens" in human history. Portuguese and Spanish priests, mostly

Jesuits and Franciscans, brought the Catholic religion to the highly cultured island of Japan in the late 1500s with great success. Tens of thousands of people converted, two seminaries were opened, native Japanese were ordained as priests, and Japan ceased to be mission territory, being elevated to a diocese. But the rising arc of missionary success just as quickly curved downward. In waves of persecutions from the 1590s through the 1640s, thousands of Catholics were persecuted, tortured, and executed until the Catholic religion, and indeed any outward expression of Christianity, was totally eradicated.

Japan almost became a Catholic nation, coming close to joining the Philippines as the only thoroughly Catholic society in Asia. Japan might have done for Asia in the 1600s what Ireland did for Europe in the early Middle Ages. It could have sent scholars, monks, and missionary priests to convert nations far larger than itself, including China. It was not to be.

Paul Miki was a native Japanese who became a Jesuit. The Jesuits would not accept into their seminary men from India or other nations who they felt were of inferior education. But the Jesuits had immense respect for the Japanese, whose culture was equal to, or even exceeded, that of Western Europe. Paul Miki was among those who, after being educated in the faith, evangelized their own people in their own language. He and others blazed a new pathway forward, allowing the Japanese to not only understand but to see, in flesh and blood, that they could retain the best of their native culture while being faithful to the newfound God of Jesus Christ.

Paul, a Jesuit brother, and his companions were the first group to suffer mass martyrdom in Japan. A military leader and adviser to the Emperor feared Spanish and Portuguese conquest of the island and ordered the arrest of six Franciscan priests and brothers, three Japanese Jesuits, sixteen other Japanese, and one Korean. The captured had their left ears mutilated and were then forced to march, bloodied, hundreds of miles to Nagasaki. On February 5, 1597, Paul and his companions were bound to crosses on a hill, like Christ, and pierced with lances. An eyewitness described the scene: "Our brother, Paul Miki, saw himself standing in the noblest pulpit he had ever filled. To his "congregation" he began by proclaiming himself a Japanese and a Jesuit... 'My religion teaches me to pardon my enemies and all who have offended me. I do gladly pardon the Emperor and all who have sought my death. I beg them to seek baptism and be Christians themselves.' Then he looked at his comrades and began to encourage them in their final struggle...Then, according to Japanese custom, the four executioners began to unsheathe their spears…The executioners killed them one by one. One thrust of the spear, then a second blow. It was over in a short time."

The executions did nothing to stop the Church. Persecution only fanned the flames of faith. By 1614 about 300,000 Japanese were Catholics. More intense persecutions followed until Japan's leaders sealed off their ports and borders from virtually all foreign penetration, a policy that lasted until the nineteenth century. Only in 1854 was Japan forcibly opened to foreign trade and Western visitors. Then, thousands of Japanese Catholics suddenly came out of hiding, mostly near Nagasaki. They bore the names of the Japanese martyrs, spoke some Latin and Portuguese, asked their new guests for statues of Jesus and Mary, and sought to verify if a French priest was legitimate with two questions: 1) Are you celibate?; and 2) Do you come from the Pope in Rome? These hidden Christians also opened their fists to show the priest something else—relics of the martyrs who their remote ancestors had honored centuries before. Their memory had never died.

Saint Paul Miki, you accepted martyrdom rather than abandon your faith. You chose to serve those closest to you rather than to flee. May we too know, love, and serve God in the heroic fashion that made you so brave and composed in the face of intense suffering.

February 8: Saint Jerome Emiliani, Priest

1481–1537

Optional Memorial; Liturgical Color: White (Violet on Lenten Weekday)

Patron Saint of orphans and abandoned children

He was forever grateful after a near-death experience

In the year 1202, a wealthy young Italian man joined the cavalry of his town's militia. The inexperienced soldiers went into battle against a neighboring town's larger force and were obliterated. Most of the retreating soldiers were run through with lances and left for dead in the mud. But at least one was spared. He was an aristocrat wearing fine clothes and new, expensive armor. He was worth taking hostage for ransom. The captive suffered in a dark, miserable prison for a full year before his father made the payment for his release. He returned to his hometown a changed man. That town was Assisi. That man was Francis.

Today's saint, Jerome Emiliani, endured much the same. He was a soldier in the city state of Venice and was appointed the commander of a fortress. In a battle against a league of city-states, the fortress fell and Jerome was imprisoned. A heavy chain was wrapped around his neck, hands, and feet, and fastened to a huge chunk of marble in an underground prison. Jerome was forgotten, alone, and treated like an animal in the gloom of a dungeon. This was the pivot point. He repented of his godless life. He prayed. He dedicated himself to the Madonna. And then, somehow, he escaped, chains in hand, and fled to a nearby city. He walked through the doors of the local church and headed to the front to fulfill a fresh vow. He slowly approached a much-venerated Virgin and placed his chains on the altar before her. He knelt, bowed his head, and prayed. His life was about to begin again.

Some pivot points can turn a life's straight line into a right angle. Other lives change slowly, bending like an arc over a long span of years. The deprivations endured by Saint Francis of Assisi and Saint Jerome Emiliani occurred suddenly. These men were healthy, had money, and were supported by family and friends. Then, shockingly, they were naked, alone, and chained. Saint Jerome could have despaired in his imprisonment. Many people do. He could have rejected God, understood his sufferings as a sign of God's disfavor, become bitter, and given up. Instead, he persevered. His imprisonment was a purification. He gave his suffering purpose.

Once free, he was like a man born anew, grateful that the heavy prison chains no longer weighed down his body to the floor. Once he started sprinting away from that prison fortress, it was like Saint Jerome never stopped running. He studied, was ordained a priest, and travelled throughout Northern Italy founding orphanages, hospitals, and homes for abandoned children, fallen women, and outcasts of all kinds. Exercising his priestly ministry in a Europe newly split by Protestant heresies, Jerome also wrote perhaps the first question-and-answer catechism in order to inculcate Catholic doctrine in his charges. Like so many saints, he seemed to be everywhere at once, caring for everyone except himself. While tending to the sick, he became infected and died in 1537, a martyr to generosity. He was, naturally, the kind of man who attracted followers. They eventually formed into a religious Congregation and received ecclesiastical approbation in 1540. Saint Jerome was canonized in 1767 and named the Patron Saint of orphans and abandoned children in 1928.

Jerome Emiliani and His Students with Mary
Cesare Ligari

Saint Jerome's life hinged on one pivot. It is a lesson. Emotional, physical, or even psychological suffering, when conquered or controlled, can be a prelude to intense gratitude and generosity. No one walks down the street more free than a former hostage. No one rests more peacefully in a warm, comfortable bed than someone who once slept on the ground. No one gulps a breath of fresh morning air quite like someone who has just heard from the doctor that the cancer is gone. Saint Jerome never lost the wonder and gratitude that flooded his heart at the moment of his liberation. All was new. All was young. The World was his. And he would place all his power and energy in God's service because he…was…a…survivor.

Saint Jerome Emiliani, you overcame confinement to live a fruitful life dedicated to God and man. Help all who are confined in any way—physically, financially, emotionally, spiritually, or psychologically—to overcome whatever binds them and to live a life without bitterness.

February 8: Saint Josephine Bakhita, Virgin

1869–1947

Optional Memorial; Liturgical Color: White (Violet on Lenten Weekday)

Patron Saint of Sudan and human-trafficking survivors

Out of Africa comes a slave, to freely serve the Master of all

Black-on-black or Arab-on-black slavery normally preceded and made possible the white-on-black slavery practiced by the colonial powers. These powers—England, France, Spain, Portugal, Italy—were not slave societies, but their colonies were. The complex, pancultural reality of the slave trade and of slavery itself was on full display in the dramatic early life of today's saint.

The future Josephine was born in Western Sudan, centuries after the Church and most Catholic nations had long since outlawed slavery. Enforcing such teachings and laws was infinitely more difficult, however, than promulgating them. And so it happened that a little African girl was kidnapped by Arab slave traders, forced to walk six hundred miles barefoot, and was then sold and resold over a twelve-year period. She was forcibly converted from her native religion to Islam, was cruelly treated by one master after another, was whipped, tattooed, and scarred. After experiencing all the humiliations inherent to captivity, she was bought by an Italian diplomat. She had been too young, and it had been too long, so she did not even know her own name when the diplomat bought her, and she had unclear recollections of where her family would be. She, essentially, had no people. The slave traders had given her the Arabic name Bakhita, "The Fortunate," and the name stuck.

Living with limited freedom as a maid with her new family, Bakhita first learned what it meant to be treated like a child of God. No chains, no lashes, no threats, no hunger. She was surrounded by the love and warmth of normal family life. When her new family was returning to Italy, she asked to accompany them, thus beginning the long second half of her life's story. Bakhita eventually settled with a different family near Venice and became the nanny for their daughter. When the parents had to tend to overseas business, Bakhita and the daughter were put in the care of local nuns. Bakhita was so edified by the sisters' prayer and charity that when her family

ST. JOSEPHINE BAKHITA

February 8

"If I were to meet the slave traders who kidnapped me and even those who tortured me I would kneel and kiss their hands, for if that did not happen, I would not be a Christian and Religious today."

returned to take her home, she refused to leave the convent, a decision reaffirmed by an Italian court which determined she had never legally been a slave in the first place. Bakhita was now absolutely free. "Freedom from" exists to make "freedom for" possible, and once free from obligations to her family, Bakhita chose to be free for service to God and her religious order. She freely chose poverty, chastity, and obedience. She freely chose not to be free. That is the opposite of slavery.

Bakhita took the name Josephine and was baptized, confirmed, and received First Holy Communion on the very same day from the Cardinal Patriarch of Venice, Giuseppe Sarto, the future Pope Saint Pius X. The same future saint received her religious vows a few years later. Saints know saints. The trajectory of Sister Josephine's life was now settled. She would remain a nun until her death. Throughout her life, Sister Josephine would often kiss the baptismal font, grateful that in its holy water she became a child of God. Her duties were humble—cooking, sewing, and greeting visitors. For a few years she travelled to other communities of her Order to share her remarkable story and to prepare younger sisters for service in Africa. One nun commented that "her mind was always on God, but her heart in Africa." Her humility, joy, and sweetness were infectious, and she became well known for her closeness to God. After heroically enduring a painful illness, she died with the words "Our Lady, Our Lady" on her lips. Her process began in 1959, and she was canonized by Pope Saint John Paul II in 2000.

Saint Josephine, you lost your freedom when young and gave it away when an adult, showing that freedom is not the goal but the pathway to serving the Master of all. From your place in heaven, give hope to those enduring the indignity of slavery and to those bound tightly by other chains.

February 10: Saint Scholastica, Virgin

c. Early Sixth Century–547
Memorial; Liturgical Color: White
(When Lenten Weekday, Optional Memorial; Violet)
Patron Saint of nuns, convulsive children, education, and books

A mysterious woman co-founds Western monasticism

Saint Scholastica was born in the decades after the last Western Emperor was forced to abandon the crumbling city of Rome in 476. Power was concentrated in the East, in Constantinople, where the real action was. Many centuries would pass until the Renaissance would cover Rome again in its classical glory. But what happened in Western Europe between the end of the Roman era in the fifth century and the dawn of the Renaissance in the fifteenth? Monasticism happened. Armies of monks founded innumerable monasteries crisscrossing the length and breadth of Europe like the beads of a rosary. These monasteries drove their roots deep into the native soil. They became centers of learning, agriculture, and culture that naturally gave birth to the dependent towns, schools, and universities which created medieval society. Monks transformed the farthest northwestern geographic protrusion of the Asian landmass into, well, Europe.

Saint Benedict and his twin sister, Saint Scholastica, are the male and female sources for that wide river of monasticism which has carved its way so deeply into the landscape of the Western world. Yet very little is known with certainty about her life. Pope Saint Gregory the Great, who reigned from 590–604, wrote about these famous twins about a half century after they died. He based his account on the testimony of abbots who personally knew Scholastica and her brother.

Gregory's biographical commentary emphasizes the warm and faith-filled closeness between the siblings. Scholastica and Benedict visited each other as often as their cloistered lives allowed. And when they met, they spoke about the things of God and the Heaven that awaited them. Their mutual affection grew out of their common love of God, showing that a correct understanding and love of God is the only source of true unity in any community, whether it be the micro-community of a family or the mega-community of an entire country. When a unified God is understood and worshipped, a unified community results.

The Benedictine monastic family tried to replicate the common knowledge and love of God which Scholastica and Benedict lived in their own family. Through common schedules, prayer, meals, singing, recreation, and work, the communities of monks who lived according to the Benedictine Rule, and who live it still, sought to replicate the well-ordered and fruitful life of a large, faith-filled family. Like a well-trained orchestra, all the monks meld their talents into an overwhelming harmony under the wand of the abbot, until their common effort swells over into the beautiful churches and music and schools that carry on today.

The gravestones in monastery cemeteries often have no names engraved on them. The polished marble may say, simply, "A holy monk." The anonymity is itself a sign of holiness. What matters is the body of the larger religious community, not the individual who was just one of that body's cells. Saint Scholastica died in 547. Her grave is known, marked, and celebrated. She is buried in a luxurious sepulchre in an underground chapel of the monastery of Monte Casino in the mountains south of Rome. She is not anonymous in her resting place, like so many monks and nuns. But she is anonymous in that so few details illustrate her character. Perhaps that was by design. Perhaps it was humility. She and her brother are major religious figures whose stamp is still impressed into Western culture. Yet she is a mystery. She is known by her legacy, and sometimes a legacy is enough. In her case, it is definitely enough.

Saint Scholastica, you established the women's branch of the Benedictine Religious Order and so gave Christian women their own communities to govern and rule. Help all who invoke your intercession to remain anonymous and humble even when developing great plans for God and His Church. You are great, and you are unknown. Help us to desire the same.

February 11: Our Lady of Lourdes

Optional Memorial; Liturgical Color: White (Violet on Lenten Weekday)
Patroness of bodily ills

A heavenly lady appears to a country girl, and miracles follow

In 1858, 14-year-old Bernadette Soubirous told her friends that a beautiful young lady was appearing to her in a rock formation on the outskirts of her small town of Lourdes. A friend asked Bernadette to do her a favor—to hold the friend's rosary in her hands the next time Bernadette knelt before the beautiful young lady. Bernadette obliged. Later, Bernadette told her friend how the lady had reacted. The lady had noticed that Bernadette was not holding her own rosary but someone else's. The lady further said she was not there to make relics and told Bernadette to return next time with her own rosary instead of another's.

Bernadette's unvarnished recounting of the lady's reaction was blunt but reasonable and, more importantly, authentic. This plainspokenness fit a pattern. Over and over again, whenever little, uneducated Bernadette was asked about the beautiful young lady she saw in the grotto, her answers never changed and included startling but authentic details. Bernadette reported that when she and the lady prayed the rosary together, the lady only said the Our Father and the Glory Be. Mary didn't pray the Hail Mary. How could she pray to herself? Would she say "Hail Me?" Bernadette reported that the lady spoke to her in the Lourdes' dialect which Bernadette herself grew up with, slightly different from standard French. Bernadette stated that a golden rose rested on each of the lady's feet. Of course! And when Bernadette respectfully asked the lady her name, she didn't understand the big words in the response: "I am the Immaculate Conception."

In addition to the miraculous cures associated with the healing waters of Lourdes, the very character of Bernadette, as well as the tone and content of her accounts, removed all doubt that the beautiful young lady she saw was indeed the Virgin Mary. Our Lady of Lourdes is perhaps the most powerful and prolific physical healer in the history of the Church after Christ himself. Through her intercession, and through the waters that flow in her magnificent shrine, many thousands have been cured of their infirmities, as medical records prove beyond any doubt. Holy Mary has appeared at various times and in various places, mostly to the simple and mostly in the country. She loves the faith of the simple and speaks to them in simple language. In this, Mary reflects the words of her Son Jesus. He speaks plainly. His message is clear. And Mary's simple words always point to the simple words of her own Son.

God is like the sun whose fiery brilliance scorches the eyes of all who look right at Him. Get too close and you'll be burned. Like the sun, the Creator of the world can be distant, mysterious, and intimidating. But Mary is like the moon, bathed in a soft, pleasant glow. She's close to us, and easy on the eyes. The sun's heat and light may make life possible, but the sun itself is dangerous and remote. But Mary can be approached by man. And like the moon, she doesn't produce her own light but just reflects in a softer tone the powerful rays of the enormous star whose light generates life itself.

Our Lady of Lourdes, give physical healing to all who invoke your intercession. The saving waters at your shrine have healed thousands of pilgrims. May all the prayers and supplications directed to you be immersed in the waters of your holy baths, so that what is asked may be granted through your intercession and according to God's will.

February 14: Saints Cyril, Monk, and Methodius, Bishop

St. Cyril: 827–869; St. Methodius: 815–884
Memorial; Liturgical Color: White
(When Lenten Weekday, Optional Memorial; Violet)
Co-Patrons of Europe and Apostles to the Slavs

Two makers of Europe light the flame of Eastern Christianity

The Cyrillic alphabet, used by hundreds of millions of people in Eastern Europe, the Balkans, and Russia, is named after today's Cyril. Numerous proofs could be advanced for why a certain person is historically significant. Few proofs, however, can eclipse an alphabet being named after you. The evangelical labors of Cyril and Methodius were so path breaking, long lasting, and culture forming that these brothers stand in the very first rank of the Church's

Saints Cyril and Methodius

greatest missionaries. Shoulder to shoulder with brave men such as Patrick, Augustine of Canterbury, Boniface, Ansgar, and others, they baptized nations, mustered clans from the forests, codified laws, transcribed alphabets, and transformed the crude pagan gropings for the divine into the transcendent worship of the one true God at Mass. Saints Cyril and Methodius helped form the religiously undivided reality of Christendom long before it was ever called Europe.

Cyril was baptized as Constantine and was known by that name until late in his life. He and Methodius were from Thessalonica, in Northern Greece, where they spoke not only Greek but also Slavonic, a critical linguistic advantage for their later missionary adventures. Cyril and Methodius received excellent educations in their youth and, as they matured, were given important educational, religious, and political appointments in an age when those disciplines were braided into one sturdy cord. The people, the state, and the Church were an undivided whole. Cyril and Methodius served the imperial court, the one true Church, and their native land as professors, governors, abbots, deacons, priests, and bishops.

Sometime after 860, the brothers were commissioned by the Emperor in Constantinople to lead a missionary crew heading into Moravia, in today's Czech Republic. They walked straight into a tangled web of political, religious, linguistic, and liturgical controversies which have vexed Eastern and Central Europe until today. The Church of Rome allowed only three languages to be used in its liturgical and scriptural texts—Hebrew, Greek, and Latin—the three languages inscribed above Christ's head on the cross. The Church in the East, juridically under Rome but culturally spinning off into its own orbit over the centuries, was a patchwork of peoples where local vernaculars were used in the liturgy. Languages are always spoken long before they are written, and the spoken Slavonic of Moravia had unique sounds demanding new letters populating a new alphabet. Cyril created that new alphabet, and then he and Methodius translated Scripture, various liturgical books, and the Mass into written Slavonic. This led to some serious tensions.

The newly Christianized German bishops were suspicious of missionaries in their own neighborhood who came from Greece, spoke Slavonic, and who celebrated the sacred mysteries in a quasi-Byzantine style. Moravia and the greater Slavic homeland were under German ecclesiastical jurisdiction, not Greek. How could the Mass be said in Slavonic, or the Gospels translated into that new language? How could a Byzantine liturgy co-exist with the Latin rite? Cyril and Methodius went to Rome to resolve these various issues with the Pope and his advisers.

The brothers were treated respectfully in Rome as well-educated and heroic missionaries. Cyril died and was buried in the Eternal City. Methodius returned to the land of the Slavs and to ongoing tensions with German ecclesiastics and princes. He translated virtually the entire Bible into Slavonic, assembled a code of Byzantine church and civil law, and firmly established, with the Pope's permission, the use of Slavonic in the liturgy. After Methodius' death, however, German and Latin Rite influences prevailed. The Byzantine Rite, the use of Slavonic in the liturgy, and the Cyrillic alphabet were all forced from Central to Eastern Europe, particularly into Bulgaria, shortly after Methodius died.

While they were always honored in the East, the Feast of SS. Cyril and Methodius was extended to the entire Catholic Church only in 1880. Pope Saint John Paul II named Saints Cyril and Methodius Co-Patrons of Europe. Their massive legacy inspires the two lungs of the Church, both East and West, to breathe more deeply the enriched oxygen of the entire Christian tradition.

Saints Cyril and Methodius, you prepared yourselves for brave and generous service to Christ and His Church through long years of preparation and, when the time came, you served heroically. May we so prepare, and so serve, until we can serve no more.

February 17: Seven Holy Founders of the Servite Order

Thirteenth Century

Optional Memorial; Liturgical Color: White (Violet on Lenten Weekday)

Invoked to aid in imitating the charity of Our Lady of Sorrows

Groups buttress fidelity to individual good intentions

There are many reasons to join a group. To quilt, play soccer, learn chess, or travel. We accomplish personal goals in a group that we would never accomplish alone. Groups create positive peer pressure to show up on time, read the book, do the exercise, or complete the task assigned. When we join a group, we freely create obligations for ourselves, because we know, deep down, that accountability to others encourages fidelity to our own obligations.

The groups of the medieval world were called guilds. Craftsmen of similar skills organized in guilds to learn, promote, and protect their trade. Guilds offered mutual assistance that no individual could replicate. There was power in numbers. Today we commemorate seven young men who belonged to a merchant guild in Florence, Italy, in the 1200s. These seven men were serious Christians. They loved God and the Church. And in addition to protecting their commercial interests by joining a guild, they also protected their souls by joining a local spiritual guild called the Confraternity of the Blessed Virgin, where their spiritual exercises were guided by a wise and educated priest who encouraged their devotion.

After the members of the Confraternity experienced mystical visions of the Virgin Mary, there was nothing left to do except abandon the world, set aside money for their families, and flee the busy city for a solitary life in the nearby mountains. The Seven fasted, prayed, and lived lives of such extreme austerity that a visiting cardinal admonished them to stop living like dogs. Over time they adopted a rule, accepted new recruits, elected leaders, and spread throughout Italy and beyond. They eventually took the name of the Order of Servants of the Blessed Virgin Mary, also known as the Servants of Mary, or Servites.

The Seven Holy Founders were especially devoted to the Seven Sorrows of Mary, and the Servites were instrumental in the Feast of Our Lady of Sorrows becoming part of the Church's calendar on September 15. The sword that pierced Mary's heart, the tears she shed when witnessing Our Lord's passion, indeed all the Sorrows of Mary motivated the Seven Holy Founders to promote devotion to Mary under this title. Mary was strong and stood at the foot of the cross. But she was also a mom who loved her boy. So she had a heavy heart that continually pondered what His suffering meant. We unite in joy at Christ's resurrection on Easter and join with Mary's sorrow just days before. The emotions of Scripture become the emotions of those who read it and those who live it in the liturgy and devotions of the Church.

The names of the Seven Holy Founders are known. But the Church celebrates them as a group, with their individuality ceding to their group identity. Together they accomplished more than seven men working separately could ever have accomplished. Their confraternity became an Order, and that Order still exists for the mutual spiritual benefit of all, a theological guild holding its members to high standards of spiritual perfection. Servite priests and brothers are still active in various countries around the world, hundreds of years after the Order's founding. This is a testament to the immovable, rock-solid foundation on which its Seven Holy Founders constructed their spiritual and theological home.

Our prayers turn to you, Seven Holy Founders of the Servite Order. Help us to find mutual support in loving God and Mary through a holy alliance with like-minded Christians. Through your example, may our love for God burn hotter than a single flame.

February 21: Saint Peter Damian, Bishop and Doctor

1007–1072

Optional Memorial; Liturgical Color: White (Violet on Lenten Weekday)

Patron Saint of Faenza and Font-Avellana, Italy

A wise monk becomes a Cardinal and thunders for reform

Every Catholic knows that the Pope is elected by, and from, the Cardinals of the Church gathered in the Sistine Chapel. Every Catholic knows that the Pope then goes to a large balcony perched high in the facade of St. Peter's Basilica to greet the faithful and receive their acceptance. This is simply the way things are done in the Church. But it's not the way things were always done. A Catholic in the early Middle Ages would have described a papal election as something like a bar room brawl, a knife fight, or a political horse race replete with bribes, connivings, and promises made just to be broken. Everyone—far-off emperors, the nobility of Rome, military generals, influential laity—tried to steer the rudder of the Church in one direction or another. Papal elections were deeply divisive and caused lasting damage to the Body of Christ. Then along came Saint Peter Damian to save the day.

Saint Peter headed a group of reform-minded Cardinals and others who decided in 1059 that only Cardinal Bishops could elect the Pope. No nobles. No crowds. No emperors. Saint Peter wrote that the Cardinal Bishops do the electing, the other clergy give their assent, and the people give their applause. This is exactly the program the Church has followed for almost a thousand years.

Today's saint sought to reform himself first, and then to pull every weed that choked life from the healthy plants in the garden of the Church. After a difficult upbringing of poverty and neglect, Peter was saved from destitution by an older brother named Damian. Out of gratitude, he added his older brother's name to his own. He was given an excellent education, in which his natural gifts became apparent, and then entered a strict monastery to live as a monk. Peter's extreme mortifications, learning, wisdom, uninterrupted life of prayer, and desire to right the ship of the Church put him into contact with many other Church leaders who desired the same. Peter eventually was called to Rome and became a counselor to a

ST. PETER DAMIAN

February 21

"Tell us, you unmanly and effeminate man, what do you seek in another male that you do not find in yourself?"

succession of popes. Against his will, he was ordained a Bishop, made a Cardinal, and headed a diocese. He fought against simony (the purchasing of church offices), against clerical marriage, and for the reform of papal elections. He also thundered, in the strongest language, against the scourge of homosexuality in the priesthood.

After being personally involved in various ecclesiastical battles for reform, he requested leave to return to his monastery. His request was repeatedly denied until finally the Holy Father let him return to a life of prayer and penance, where his primary distraction was carving wooden spoons. After fulfilling a few more sensitive missions to France and Italy, Peter Damian died of fever in 1072. Pope Benedict XVI has described him as "one of the most significant figures of the eleventh century...a lover of solitude and at the same time a fearless man of the Church, committed personally to the task of reform." He died about one hundred years before Saint Francis of Assisi was born, yet some have referred to him as the Saint Francis of his age.

More than two hundred years after our saint's death, Dante wrote his Divine Comedy. The author is guided through paradise and sees a golden ladder, lit by a sunbeam, stretching into the clouds above. Dante begins to climb and meets a soul radiating the pure love of God. Dante is in awe that the heavenly choirs have fallen silent to listen to this soul speak: "The mind is light here, on earth it is smoke. Consider, then, how it can do down there what it cannot do up here with heaven's help." God is unknowable even in heaven itself, so how much more unfathomable must He be on earth. Dante drinks in this wisdom and, transfixed, asks this soul its name. The soul then describes its prior earthly life: "In that cloister I became so steadfast in the service of our God that with food seasoned just with olive-juice lightheartedly I bore both heat and cold, content with thoughtful prayers of contemplation. I was, in that place, Peter Damian." Dante is among refined company in the loftiest ranks of heaven with today's saint.

Saint Peter Damian, you never asked of others what you did not demand of yourself. You even endured the detraction and calumny of your peers. Help us to reform others by our example, learning, perseverance, mortifications, and prayers.

February 22: Chair of Saint Peter, Apostle

Feast; Liturgical Color: White

The gift of authority serves order and truth in the Church

It's unusual to have a feast day for a chair. When we think of a chair, perhaps we think of a soft recliner into which our body sinks as if into a warm bath. Or our mind turns to a classroom chair, a chair in a waiting room, or one at a restaurant. But the chair the Church commemorates today is more like the heroic-sized marble chair which holds the giant body of President Lincoln in the Lincoln Memorial. We commemorate today a chair like the judge's in a courtroom or that unique high-backed chair called a throne. These are not ordinary chairs. They are seats of authority and judgment. They hold power more than people. We stand before them while their occupants sit. Judges and kings retire or die, but chairs and thrones remain to hold their successors. The Nicene Creed even describes Jesus as "seated" at God's right hand. The fuller, symbolic meaning of the word "chair" is what today's feast commemorates.

Against the farthest wall of Saint Peter's Basilica in Rome is not a statue of Saint Peter, as one might imagine, but a heroic-sized sculpture framing a chair. To celebrate the Chair of St. Peter is to celebrate the unity of the Church. The chair is a symbol of Saint Peter's authority, and that authority is not meant for conquest like military power. Ecclesiastical authority is directed toward unity.

Jesus Christ could have gathered an unorganized group of disciples united only by their common love of Him. He didn't. He could have written the Bible Himself, handed it to His followers, and said, "Obey this text." He didn't. Jesus called to Himself, by name, twelve men. He endowed them with the same powers He possessed and left this organized band of brothers as an identifiable, priestly fraternity specifically commissioned to baptize and to preach. In North Africa at the time of Saint Augustine, twelve co-consecrating bishops were canonically required at the ordination of a bishop, mirroring "The Twelve" called by Christ. What a profound liturgical custom! Today the Church requires only three co-consecrators.

What is even more striking about Christ's establishment of an orderly Church structure is its double organizing principle. The Twelve's headship over the many is itself subjected to the headship of Saint Peter. He is the keeper of the keys, the rock upon which the Lord built His Church. This all makes sense. What good would a constitution be without a Supreme Court to adjudicate disputes over its interpretation? Any authoritative text needs a living body to stand over it to arbitrate, interpret, and define, with authority equal to the text itself, any and all misinterpretations, confusions, or honest disputes. Just as a constitution needs a court, the Bible needs a Magisterium. And that Magisterium, in turn, needs a head as well.

The authority of the papal office, doctrinally, is a negative charism preserving the Church from teaching error. It is not a guarantee that the pope will teach, explain, or live the faith perfectly. Christ guaranteed that the gates of hell would not prevail against the Church. That's a negative promise. But this promise also prophesies that the Office of Peter will be a lightning rod absorbing strikes from the forces of evil, that this Church, and no other, will be the target of the darkest of powers. A real Church has real enemies.

The Church has never had an Office of Saint Paul. When the person of Paul disappeared, so did his specific role. But the Office of Peter continues, as does the Office of all the Apostles. In other words, the Church has both a foundation and a structure built on that foundation. And authority in that structure is not transmitted personally, from father to son or from one family to the next. Authority attaches to the Office of St. Peter and endows its occupant with the charisms promised by Christ to Saint Peter. And this charism will endure until the sun sets for the last time. As long as there is a Church, it will teach objective truth guaranteed by objective leadership. And that leadership, symbolized in the Chair of St. Peter, is directed toward unity. One Lord. One faith. One Shepherd. One flock. The united fabric of the Church, so fought for, so torn, so necessary, is what we honor today.

God in Heaven, we thank You for the ordered community of faith we enjoy in the Church. Saint Peter guided the early Church and guides Her still, ensuring that we remain one, holy, catholic, and apostolic until the end of time. Continue to grace Your Church with the unity so necessary to accomplish Her mission on earth.

February 23: Saint Polycarp, Bishop and Martyr

c. 69–c. 155

Memorial; Liturgical Color: Red

(When Lenten Weekday, Optional Memorial; Violet)

Patron Saint of earache sufferers

A venerable bishop's martyrdom ends the sub-apostolic age

A Catholic bishop is brutally executed in Turkey. His assassin yells "Allahu Akbar," stabs his victim repeatedly in the heart, and then cuts his head off. There are witnesses to the act. The few local priests and faithful fear for their lives. The Pope in Rome is shocked and prays for the deceased. Five thousand people attend the solemn funeral Mass. An event from long ago? No.

The murdered bishop was an Italian Franciscan named Luigi Padovese, the mourning Pope was Benedict XVI, and the year was 2010. Turkey is dangerous territory for a Catholic bishop, whether he is Bishop Padovese or today's saint, Bishop Polycarp. For over a millennium, the Anatolian Peninsula was the cradle of Eastern Christianity. That era has long since come to a close. A few hundred miles and one thousand eight hundred years separate, or perhaps unite, Bishop Padovese with Bishop Polycarp. Whether shed by the sharp knife of a modern Muslim fanatic or spilled by a sword swung by a pagan Roman soldier, the blood still ran red from the neck of a Christian leader, puddling in the dirt of a hostile land.

The news of the martyrdom of Saint Polycarp, Bishop of Smyrna, spread far and wide in his own time, making him as famous in the early Church as he is now. He was martyred around 155 A.D., one of the few early martyrs whose death is verified by documentation so precise that it even proves that he was executed on the exact day of his present feast—February 23. Polycarp was eighty-six years old when a rash of persecution broke out against the local Church. He waited patiently at a farm outside of town for his executioners to come and knock on his door. He was then brought before a Roman magistrate and ordered to reject his atheism. Imagine that. What an interesting twist! The Christian is accused of atheism by the pagan "believer." Such was the Roman perspective. Christians were atheists because they rejected the ancient civic religion which had been believed by everyone, everywhere, and always.

The Roman gods were more patriotic symbols than objects of belief. No one was martyred for believing in them. No one fought over their creeds, because there were no creeds. These gods did for Rome what flags, national hymns, and civic holidays do for a modern nation. They united it. They were universal symbols of national pride. Just as everyone stands for the national anthem, faces the flag, puts their hand over their heart, and sings the familiar words, so too did Roman citizens walk up the wide marble steps of their many-columned temples, make a petition, and then burn incense on the altar of their favorite god.

It required heroic courage for Polycarp, and thousands of other early Christians, to not drop some grains of incense into a flame burning before a pagan god. For the Romans, to not burn such incense was akin to spitting on a flag. But Polycarp simply refused to renounce the truth of what he had heard as a young man from the mouth of Saint John: that a carpenter named Jesus, who had lived a few weeks to the south of Smyrna, had risen from the dead after His cold, linen-wrapped body had been placed in a guarded tomb. And this had happened recently, in the time of Polycarp's own grandparents!

Polycarp was proud to die for a faith he had adopted through hard-earned thought. His pedigree as a Christian leader was impeccable. He had learned the faith from one of the Lord's very own Apostles. He had met the famous Bishop of Antioch, Saint Ignatius, when Ignatius passed through Smyrna on the way to his execution in Rome. One of Saint Ignatius' famous seven letters is even addressed to Polycarp. Polycarp, Saint Irenaeus of Lyon tells us, even travelled to Rome to meet with the Pope over the question of the dating of Easter. Irenaeus had known and had learned from Polycarp when Irenaeus was a child in Asia Minor. Polycarp's own letter to the Philippians was read in churches in Asia as if it were part of Scripture, at least until the fourth century.

It was this venerable, grey-haired man, the last living witness to the apostolic age, whose hands were bound behind him to a stake, and who stood "like a mighty ram" as thousands screamed for his blood. Bishop Polycarp nobly accepted what he had not actively sought. He was stabbed to death after the flames licking his aged skin failed to consume him. His body was burned after his death, and the faithful preserved his bones, the first instance of relics being so honored. A few years after Polycarp's death, a man from Smyrna named Pionius was martyred for observing the martyrdom of Saint Polycarp. In just this fashion links are added, one after another, to the chain of faith which stretches down the centuries to the present, where we honor Saint Polycarp as if we were seated within earshot of the action in the stadium that fateful day.

Great martyr Saint Polycarp, make us steadfast witnesses to the truth in word and deed, just as you witnessed to the truth in your own life and death. Through your intercession, make our commitment to our religion a life project, enduring until our life of faith concludes with a death of faith.

February 27: St. Gregory of Narek, Abbot and Doctor

950–c. 1003

Optional Memorial: Liturgical Color: White

Widely venerated in Armenia

A mystical eastern monk praises God like a troubadour

A crowning glory of the Armenian people is that their nation was the first to adopt Christianity as its official religion. Approximately twelve years before the Roman Emperor Constantine legalized Christianity in 313, an Armenian King converted to Christianity. Following the universal custom of mankind, the King's religion then became his people's. Though the actual conversion of individual souls required decades of subsequent evangelical effort, this early baptism of an entire nation has granted the Armenian Apostolic Church unique status as the custodian of Armenian national identity. Living proof of Armenia's ancient Christian pedigree is found in the old city of Jerusalem. An Armenian patriarch, cathedral, and seminary anchor the peaceful Armenian Quarter, one of the four neighborhoods packed behind the walls of the city where it all began.

Today's saint, Gregory of Narek, was a mediaeval Armenian monk who wrote mystical poetry, hymns, and biblical commentaries. He is one of Armenia's greatest literary figures and poets. His principal work, the "Book of Lamentations" consists of ninety-five prayers he composed as an encyclopedia of prayer for all people. The twentieth-century Catechism of the Catholic Church notes that while Western Medieval piety developed the rosary as a lay substitute for praying the Psalms, the Armenian tradition developed hymns and songs to Mary as the primary expression of popular piety, as seen in the works of St. Gregory of Narek (CCC #2678). Pope Saint John Paull II also referenced St. Gregory in his encyclical on Mary, *Redemptoris Mater*: "…with powerful poetic inspiration (St. Gregory) ponders the…mystery of the Incarnation, …an occasion to sing and extol the extraordinary dignity and magnificent beauty of the Virgin Mary, Mother of the Word made flesh."

Like St. Ephrem, a centuries-earlier Syrian archetype of Eastern monasticism, St. Gregory uses metaphor, songs, litanies, and poetry to communicate Christian truth. The Western tradition, especially since the time of St. Augustine, tends to communicate the truths of Christianity in less artistic ways - through close reasoning, apologetics, the synthesis of Greek philosophy with Christian doctrine, and by showing the internal harmony of Scriptural texts.

The Armenian Christian tradition, like related ancient churches born near the cradle of mankind, has not sharpened its sword of thought by constant clashing with enemy metal, as has occurred in the West. The benefits of a monoculture - of a people who all speak the same language, kneel before the same God, profess the same faith, and sing the same songs – is deep unity. A monoculture has no need to hone arguments. When everyone agrees on the fundamentals, when the tapestry of a culture is not torn or frayed, the writer, priest, poet, composer, or monk can sing, whistle, ruminate, and dream like a madman or a troubadour. When he describes a rainbow as God's bow in the sky, hears the sweet voice of Mary in a lark, imagines a devilish monster lurking in the wine-dark sea, or is convinced that the blood dripping from the side of Christ soaks and sanctifies the earth itself, the faithful quietly nod in agreement and humbly whisper: "Thus it is. Thus it shall always be."

Little is known of the life of St. Gregory of Narek other than that he was a dedicated monk who lived his entire adult life in a monastery situated in todays' eastern Turkey, in the Armenian homeland between the Black and Caspian Seas. St. Gregory's essence is truly to be found in the spaces between his words. He *is* his writings. St. Gregory was never formally canonized, a not uncommon fact for holy men and women of his era. During a Mass in 2015 commemorating the hundredth anniversary of the Armenian genocide by the Ottoman Turks, Pope Francis declared St. Gregory of Narek a Doctor of the Church, the thirty-sixth person so honored and only the second from the churches of the East.

Surprisingly, St. Gregory was not a Catholic, though he did pertain to an apostolic church with legitimate sacraments and a hierarchical structure which, however, is not in formal communion with Rome. The narrow theological arteries that run east from Constantinople become thinner as they spread ever eastward, often terminating in ecclesiastical cardiac arrest – in churches without people, in thrones without bishops, in altars without sacrifices, and in monasteries without monks. It is one of the holy obligations of the still robust Roman Church to exalt those whom others cannot, to witness to beauty wherever it may be found, and to call Christian leaders to gather in the immensity of St. Peter's Basilica to anoint the memory of a gifted Christian of long ago with the noble title of doctor.

St. Gregory of Narek, your quiet, humble, and hidden life produced a rich garden of poems and prayers. May your redolent words and rich images fire our imaginations and inflame our hearts so that our flame of faith burns as hot as yours in its love for Christ and Mary.

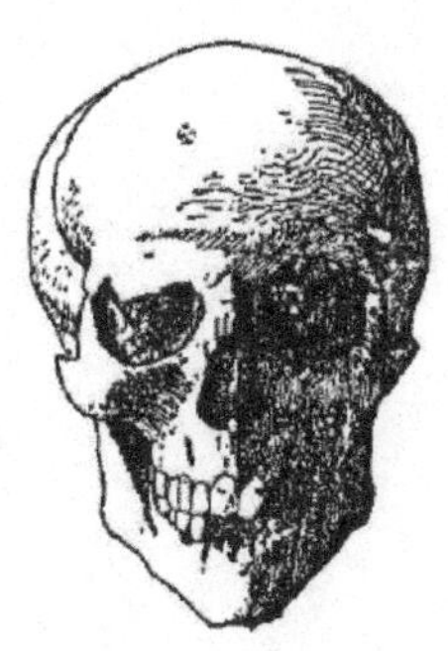

MARCH

"Greetings, favored one!" Lk 1:28

March 3: Saint Katharine Drexel, Virgin (U.S.A.)

1858–1955

Optional Memorial; Liturgical Color: White (Violet when Lenten Weekday)

Patron Saint of racial justice and philanthropists

From riches to rags, she lived the Catholic dream

Today's saint wove in and out of oncoming traffic. She travelled north while everyone else was zooming south. Friends and acquaintances in her refined, educated, upper-class milieu glided past her in search of marriage, children, wealth, travel, security, and leisure. Katharine deftly avoided them and moved forward at her own deliberate pace, looking for poverty, chastity, obedience, solitude, and God. She turned down a marriage proposal, rejected a life of luxury, and resisted the expectations of her status. Katharine was deeply rooted in all things Catholic from her youth. She went from riches to rags, starting out immensely wealthy yet becoming progressively poorer with age. The classic American story is to begin with little, work hard, identify opportunity, live frugally, and ultimately attain success through sheer dint of effort. Saint Katharine Drexel's father was immensely wealthy and powerful. He lived, even embodied, the American dream. His daughter lived the Catholic dream.

One of the reasons why Saint Katharine ever became a nun in the first place was because a Pope did his job. In 1887, Katharine and her two sisters went to Rome and were received in audience by Pope Leo XIII. Having come into enormous inheritances upon their father's recent death, the young ladies were financially supporting some Indian missions in the American West. Katharine asked the Holy Father if he could send some missionaries to staff these missions. The Pope responded like a wise and zealous priest. He asked Katharine to send herself. That is, he asked her to consider consecrating her own life to Christ as a missionary sister. The Pope's words were a turning point. She sought spiritual counsel from trusted priests and saw the path forward. In 1889, her local newspaper ran the headline: "Miss Drexel Enters a Catholic Convent—Gives Up Seven Million."

ST. KATHARINE DREXEL

March 3

"The Eucharist is a never-ending sacrifice. It is the Sacrament of love, the supreme love, the act of love."

From that point on, Sister Katharine Drexel never stopped giving. Saint Teresa of Ávila said that one man and God make an army. With Saint Katharine Drexel, one woman and a fortune made an army. She founded an order, the Sisters of the Blessed Sacrament, with the counsel and encouragement of Saint Mother Cabrini. Her order began over a hundred missions and schools for American Indians and African Americans in the American South and West, including one of the first universities to admit racial minorities. Katharine was decades ahead of the civil rights movement which caught fire in the U.S. in the decade after her death. Sister Katharine spent a good part of her life on trains, travelling at least six months every year to visit her apostolates and the sisters who staffed them. Yet amid all this activity, she maintained an intense life of prayer. In this she emulated the balance typical of the greatest saints. Their concern for justice, not social justice, was rooted in a deep love of God present in the Blessed Sacrament. There was no duality in this. It wasn't social work on one side and the sacraments and devotion on the other side. It was contemplation in action, love of God overflowing naturally into love of neighbor.

After a life of generous self-gift, Saint Katharine suffered a major heart attack and spent the last twenty years of her life largely immobile, in prayer before the Blessed Sacrament. She had always retained the desire to become a contemplative, and it was granted, in a sense, in her last two decades. She died at a venerable age and was canonized by Pope Saint John Paul II in 2000. Saint John Neumann, the Bishop of Philadelphia who died just two years after Katharine was born in his diocese, was a poor immigrant who embodied the best of the first wave of immigrant Catholicism in the U.S. Katharine embodied a succeeding generation of homegrown Catholicism. She was an icon of a new era of Catholic Americans who would power the incredibly organized and vibrant early and mid-twentieth century Church in the U.S: Catholic educated, socially conscious, pope-friendly, sacramentally focused, wealthy, and very generous. Saint Katharine lived and died a model nun.

Saint Katharine Drexel, intercede for all who love inordinately the things of this world. Your holy detachment from wealth and comfort freed you for a life dedicated to prayer and service. May we have that same detachment and that same commitment to God.

March 4: Saint Casimir

1458–1484

Optional Memorial; Liturgical Color: White (Violet when Lenten Weekday)

Patron Saint of Poland and Lithuania

A prince crowned with humility lives well but not long

Ever since the Three Kings left their gifts at the altar of the crib in Bethlehem, Jesus Christ, King of the Universe, has drawn generations of nobles, kings, and emperors to Himself. Today we commemorate a young man named Casimir, Prince of Poland, who died at the age of twenty-five. Casimir was the third child in a family of thirteen siblings who had everything that life could offer. But it was still not enough, and Casimir knew it. Unlike many wealthy, powerful, educated people, Casimir knew that life did not offer, and could not offer, what the soul most deeply yearned for. He had his head screwed on straight and tight. Casimir never lost sight of the higher things that truly mattered, even though his life was full of the intrigues and cares of war and state.

Any true search is open to finding. A search that begins with the premise that it will never find, or never end, is not really a search. It's just wandering. A true searcher must be a finder. How many people claim to be searching for the truth, for God, for meaning! Yet when they unearth the elusive treasure, open it up, and see its contents, they are disappointed and move along to search for something else. Why? Perhaps because the treasure made moral demands on them or required that prior life decisions be repudiated or modified. If a searcher sets personal conditions on what he will find, his search will never end. The search will just become a reflection of the searcher's own personality and desires, not a true quest for something objective outside of himself.

Saint Casimir searched for God as a child, as all youth do. But his search unearthed a treasure early on. What Casimir sought, Poland provided. Casimir imbued so totally what his Catholic birthplace offered that he is considered an emblematic Polish prince: pious, just, chaste, poor, and strong. A country, similar to a religion, is a carrier of meaning. It absorbs and refines, over time, millions of individual searches until it responds to its people's searches in the form of heroes, flags, hymns, holidays, and statues. A patriot loves his country in the same way that a religious man loves his religion and God. His love is specific. He loves *a* country, *a* religion, and *a* God—and Casimir was no exception.

It is said that behind every great man is a great woman. Saint Casimir never married and preserved his chastity until death, despite offers of marriage. What was behind him was not a great woman but a great nation. Poland was his mistress. The faith and thick traditions of Poland developed over many centuries in response to man's search for meaning in that great nation. The Polish nation did not understand Poland's past as an anchor, an imposition, or a burden. Poles understood their nation's cultural riches as a common inheritance of their ancestors. And Poles were eager to honor their forefathers by faithfully accepting, with gratitude, what they handed down.

The fullness of these traditions was imparted to today's saint from a young age by his teachers, especially by learned priests who were like second fathers to him. Casimir learned to love the Lord's Passion, the Sacraments, the Virgin, and the Church. These loves deepened as he matured and personally experienced the harshness and venality of life at court and on the march. He did not need to become a priest or religious in order to live his faith. He remained a layman his entire brief life. In this he presaged the emphasis on lay vocations the Church would promote in the twentieth century. He was a layman, a prince, and a saint. Anything is possible in the Church for those who love God first and foremost.

Saint Casimir, we ask your intercession to aid all leaders of governments, churches, and families to emulate your virtues; to be poor in spirit, just, pure, and faithful. With your aid, may leaders guide those under their authority to love and serve their country and their God with greater fervor.

March 7: Saints Perpetua and Felicity, Martyrs

c. Late Second Century–203
Memorial; Liturgical Color: Red
(When Lenten Weekday, Optional Memorial; Violet)
Patron Saints of expectant mothers, widows, and butchers

They bled to death as pagan eyes drank in the spectacle

Many centuries ago in the desert lands of North Africa, now populated by millions of the adherents of Islam, there was once a thriving Catholic Church. Dioceses, bishops, theologians, shrines, schools, monasteries, convents, and saints filled the towns hugging the southern coast of the Mediterranean Sea. This vibrant Catholicism generated, and was inspired by, the witness of numerous martyrs. Many of their names are known, among them today's saints, Felicity and Perpetua. Few documents in Church history can match the raw power of the first-person, eye-witness narrative of the passion of Perpetua and Felicity. It is a gripping account filled with breathtaking dramatic detail. The reader can almost feel the hot sand of the arena warming his feet, a gentle sea breeze caressing his cheeks, and the sweaty crowd pressing against him, their roar for blood echoing through the dry air.

Vivia Perpetua, twenty-two years old, was married, a noblewoman, and a new mother whose baby was still nursing. Her pagan father begged his favorite daughter to renounce her Christian faith, but to no avail. Felicity was a slave and pregnant when jailed. She gave birth a few days before her martyrdom. Her child would be raised by Christian women in Carthage. Perpetua, in her own hand, recorded the events leading up to her martyrdom, while an eyewitness to her death completed the text later.

When they were first thrown into the arena, Perpetua and Felicity were attacked by a rabid heifer, which was chosen because it shared the same sex as its victims. The young women were grievously injured by the mad cow and then momentarily removed from the arena until gladiators were brought in to conclude the day's spectacle. The executioners carried out their duties quickly, though Perpetua had to guide the gladiator's sword to her throat after he first painfully struck a bone instead of a vein. As the narration states, "Perhaps such a woman...could not die unless she herself had willed it." Saints Perpetua and Felicity were imprisoned together, suffered together, and died together in 203 A.D. in Carthage, North Africa, along with other noble martyrs whose names are preserved in the same account.

The vivid description of their deaths was so moving that it was faithfully preserved down through the centuries and has come to us largely intact. Apart from the New Testament writings themselves, only a few documents from the early Church pre-date the passion narrative of Perpetua and Felicity. It invites tantalizing reflection on how many similar firsthand testimonies of famous martyrdoms from the early Church have been lost! What could have been known about the final moments of Saints Paul, Cecilia, Agatha, and so many apostles and popes! The accounts of Perpetua, Felicity, and Polycarp must fire our imagination for all the rest. The Church in North Africa so often read the account of Perpetua and Felicity in its public liturgies that Saint Augustine, a North African bishop living two hundred years after their martyrdoms, had to remind his faithful that the narrative was not on a par with Scripture itself.

The fact that women and slaves, both mothers who loved their children, were willing to die rather than renounce their faith, testifies to the revolutionary message of Jesus Christ. He gave us a true religion. But He also gave us a true anthropology. He has revealed to man his true origins, his high dignity, and his ultimate purpose. Jesus reveals man to himself. So when early Christians, or present-day Christians, understand that they are made in God's image and likeness, and that His Son died for them as much as He died for anyone else, they stand a little taller. If a Christian is told he is garbage, property, a slave, old, a prisoner, or a foreigner, he shouldn't flinch at the insult, because under such denigrations is a deeper identity: "child of God," "made in God's image and likeness," and "worthy of the blood of the Lamb." These are the titles of a citizen of the Kingdom of God, whose shadow covers the earth and comforts all those who live in its shade. Felicity and Perpetua clung to their identity as Christians in the face of imprisonment, ridicule, torture, and pain. The newness of the faith, and the dignity it imparted, fortified them to accept death rather than a return to rough paganism. May our faith be as fresh to us.

Saints Felicity and Perpetua, your martyrdom was an act of bravery, which moved the Christians of your age and continues to move us today. Give all who invoke your names similar courage, fortitude, and faith to overcome timidity in witnessing to Christ in difficult circumstances.

March 8: Saint John of God, Religious

1495–1550

Optional Memorial; Liturgical Color: White (Violet when Lenten Weekday)

Patron Saint of hospitals, printers, the sick, and alcoholics

He walked the fine line between madness and holiness

There are many "Johns" who are saints, beginning with those found in Scripture itself: Saint John the Baptist, Saint John the Evangelist, Saint John of the Cross, Saint John Fisher, etc. The name John has also been taken by many popes. Today's John has the title "of God." It is a simple and direct title. The word "God" conveys everything under God and everything that is God, without distinctions such as "of the Cross," "of the Holy Name," or "of the Infant Jesus." Neither does it carry any hint of a homeland such as "of Assisi," "of Calcutta," or "of Padua." All saints are "of God," of course, but the plain title "of God" fits the personality, outlook, education, and simplicity of today's John very well. The name was not given to him posthumously. John said that the Infant Jesus gave him the name in a dream. A Spanish Bishop who personally knew John and his work ordered him to bear this appellation once he knew its divine origins.

Saint John of God did not have the advantage of an excellent education. But what his mind lacked his heart supplied. He left his Portuguese home as a child in the care of a priest and went to neighboring Spain. From there he lived an itinerant life as a farmer, shepherd, adventurer, and then soldier. He travelled the length and breadth of Europe fighting in the service of kings and princes, mostly against Muslim Turks. Many years later he found his way back home and went to see if his parents were still alive. But he had been gone so long, and had left so young, that he could not even remember their names. An uncle told him that they had died. At this point, the wandering John decided to ransom his own freedom to North African Muslims in exchange for Christian hostages. The

ST. JOHN OF GOD

March 8

"Whenever I see so many poor brothers and neighbors of mine suffering beyond their strength and overwhelmed with so many physical or mental ills which I cannot alleviate, then I become exceedingly sorrowful; but I trust in Christ, who knows my heart. And so I say, 'Woe to the man who trusts in men rather than in Christ.'"

plan came to nothing and he returned to Southern Spain.

At this, the lowest point of his aimless life, John had a breakthrough, or perhaps a breakdown. He was selling religious books from town to town when he fell under the influence of a saint, John of Ávila. Saints know saints. Upon hearing John of Ávila preach about the martyr Saint Sebastian, and upon receiving his advice in spiritual direction, the wandering John stopped in his tracks. He fasted, he prayed, and he went on pilgrimage to the Shrine of Our Lady of Guadalupe in Extremadura, Spain. So total was his repentance for his past sins that he was placed for a time in a hospital for the mentally ill. But his repentance was real. He changed forever and always and started caring for the kind of person that he used to be.

John somehow raised enough money to start a small hospital and thus began, in an orderly and professional manner, to care for the sick, feed the hungry, clothe the naked, convert the sinner, and shelter the homeless and orphans. He had no equal in giving of himself to his patients, and his reputation for holiness spread across Spain. He gave away his cloaks so often that his Bishop had a habit made, ordered John to put it on, and told him not to give it away. John's total dedication to the poor and sick drew many followers. They emulated his generosity, and soon an Order was born. The group was eventually approved by the Holy See in 1572 under the title The Brothers Hospitallers of Saint John of God. The Order spread quickly throughout the world, often with the support of the Spanish Crown. Its work on behalf of the poor continues today in numerous countries through hundreds of institutions.

Saint John of God practiced a type of Ignatian spirituality in evaluating his own life. But he was not just a spectator of his life, observing it from the outside. He became a student of himself, evaluated his own errors, listened to advice, stopped what he was doing, changed direction, and charted a new course in middle age. He was, in modern terms, a "late vocation." He cared little for his own physical health and died on his fifty-fifth birthday while kneeling in prayer before an altar in his room. In some saints there is a fine line between sanctity and madness. Saint John of God straddled that fine line. He became mad for the Lord and was canonized by the Church for his holy madness in serving the poor and the God who loves them.

Saint John of God, help us to follow your example of service to the poor through gift of self. You did not just ask for charitable donations but for charity itself. You did not ask others to do what you did not do yourself. Through your intercession, may all those in need encounter a servant as generous as yourself to satisfy their basic needs.

March 9: Saint Frances of Rome, Religious

1384–1440

Optional Memorial; Liturgical Color: White (Violet when Lenten Weekday)

Patron Saint of motorists and widows

Just to be near her was thought a blessing

Today's saint, born into a wealthy noble family in the Eternal City, was married to a man from a similarly privileged family when she was just thirteen. Saint Frances earnestly sought to do the will of God in serving her husband, her children, and her home while also attempting to live a high level of holiness modeled on the life of a nun. She had desired to enter religious life from a young age, but her father refused to break his promise to give Frances in marriage to a fellow nobleman. Frances struggled with an internal conflict between her married state and the religious state to which she had originally felt called. This was not a choice between a good and a bad option. It was a natural tension in the soul of a holy woman who saw two paths open before her, both of which led to God. After her husband died and her children were grown, Saint Frances did live the ordered life of a religious, albeit outside of a convent.

The divine pull that Saint Frances felt in the direction of two callings was not unusual. Other saints before her had been wives and mothers before becoming religious. The theology of the Church in the twentieth century, ratified by the teachings of the Second Vatican Council, now offers a vision of holiness which resolves much of this tension in trying to discern a vocation. The primary calling of all Christians is imparted through Baptism, fortified in Confirmation, and nourished in reception of Holy Communion. These Sacraments are sufficient armor to fit one for holiness in any and all circumstances. The married life and its natural domestic concerns are, then, as much a theater for holiness as a cloister.

The Church wants all Catholics to understand daily life as its own drama in fulfilling, or rejecting, God's will. It is not that one is distracted with the details of work, family, domestic chores, and children while the real action takes place in the parish, the monastery, the retreat center, or the convent. The real action is at home, in the domestic church. It is precisely at home where Christians spend most of their time, raise their children, engage with their spouses, and accomplish the multitude of tasks that make life happen. Home and work are not spheres of life. They are life. And it would be absurd to argue that the will of God lies outside of life itself. To say that holiness is for everyone is to say that all of creation is a forum to pursue it, and that no vocation limits the opportunity to accomplish God's will.

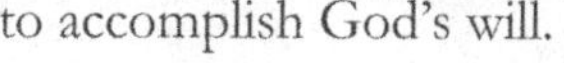

Saint Frances of Rome was a model wife and mother for forty years, often in violent and difficult circumstances provoked by skirmishes related to the Western Schism, the era of more than one pope which divided Rome's elites into warring factions. Frances' husband loved and revered her, her servants admired her, and her children adored her. In addition to performing her domestic duties so faithfully, Frances also fasted, prayed, had a vibrant mystical spirituality, and was generous with the poor. Her charity toward the destitute was not the modern charity of making charitable donations. She did the work, not someone else. She herself made personal contact with the homeless, the hungry, and beggars. Her sterling example of piety and service led her to found a group of like-minded women who lived in the world but who bound themselves to a life of prayer and service. The group was later recognized as an Order in the Church under the title the Oblates of Saint Frances of Rome. So, in addition to fulfilling her own duties, Frances also helped similarly high-placed women to avoid lives of frivolousness and mundanity.

Saint Frances of Rome was generous in all things, saw her guardian angel at her side for many years, ate little more than dry bread, and had a provable gift of healing. As her reputation for holiness spread in her later years, to be in her mere presence was considered a blessing by the people of Rome. As wife, mother, and later Oblate, she stretched herself to the limit in seeking out and doing God's will, precisely as that will was transmitted to her by the Church she loved with such fervor.

Saint Frances of Rome, through your intercession, aid all wives and mothers to live lives of generous service to their families. Help them to serve the domestic Church by creating, and fortifying, that cradle of holiness and culture the Church so needs to flourish.

March 17: Saint Patrick, Bishop

Fifth Century

Optional Memorial; Liturgical Color: Violet (Lenten Weekday)

Patron Saint of Ireland

The black arts of pagandom bowed to this one-man fortress

Today's saint, the Patron of Ireland, was English. He was born in an unknown year to Catholic parents in an educated home in Roman Britain. His father was a deacon and his grandfather a married priest. When he first went to Ireland, he did not go willingly. He was kidnapped by pirates at the age of sixteen and enslaved. He went from the warm embrace of his home to herding pigs, exposed to sleet and cold, starving on the rain-soaked coast of rural Ireland. Times of great danger and deprivation are often times of great grace. In young Patrick's years of isolation, cold, hunger, and loss, prayer was his only nourishment and comfort. His captivity turned a boy into a man and transformed a tepid Christian into an ardent soul burning with love for the Holy Trinity.

After six years of torturous enslavement, Patrick escaped his captors and made the difficult voyage back to his own nation, family, and language. But the Irish were never far from his mind. One night, he had a dream. Patrick sees a man he knew in Ireland named Victoricus approaching from the west. Victoricus holds countless letters and hands one to Patrick. It is titled "The Voice of the Irish." As he begins to read the letter, Patrick hears a multitude of voices rising, as if one, from a forest near the Western Sea: "We beg you, holy youth, to come and walk among us once more." Patrick is deeply moved. Unable to read any more, he wakes up.

Patrick decides to be a slave of Christ and to return as a missionary to Ireland. Feeling himself unprepared, he first studies for many years at monasteries in France. After receiving an excellent education in the faith, he receives priestly and episcopal ordination. He then embarks as a fully equipped missionary for his adopted homeland. There he finds a rustic people steeped in paganism. It is not today's paganism—well read, superior, and too sophisticated to believe in religious "mythology." Real paganism, the paganism of remote Ireland, called upon dark forces to conquer the white spirits and angels of God. Real paganism casts spells, calls down lightning from the night sky, mixes potions to poison its enemies, and forms flames into swords for battle. Real paganism invokes the devil because it knows Satan keeps his appointments. This is the dark paganism Patrick finds lurking in the foggy hills and bogs of his new land. Fifth-century Ireland had a deeply entrenched, richly layered culture of pagan worship. And Bishop Patrick used his crozier, like a dagger, to stab it right in the heart.

Saint Patrick converted the Irish, one tribe after another. He matched the tribes' preternatural forces with supernatural powers. There are numerous anecdotes, of dubious historicity, describing how Patrick turned an enemy into a fox, converted his walking staff into a tree, or drove all the snakes out of Ireland. These tales illustrate a deeper point—Saint Patrick had command over creation itself and used that power to communicate the truth of the Christian God who created creation. There is no doubt that Saint Patrick harvested an immense number of souls.

For the Church to send a bishop to Ireland in the fifth century was to land a man on the moon. Beyond Ireland there was no one and nothing. Patrick evangelized a rugged, clever people in a rugged, clever way. He conquered their witches, wizards, and warlocks with the Holy Spirit. He vanquished their incantations, potions, demons, and sorcery with a powerful brew, the Body and Blood, Soul and Divinity of the Son of God in the Mystery of the Altar we call the Blessed Sacrament. He overcame the "black laws of pagandom" with a protecting God who walks always and lovingly at our side.

Many centuries of saints, abbots, missionaries, scholars, and monks set sail from tiny Ireland to traverse the globe in service of the Gospel. They owe the rich Catholic culture of their homeland to that mighty pillar of faith known as Saint Patrick.

Saint Patrick, Apostle of Ireland, assist us through your intercession to trust in the raw power of God to conquer evil. Give us confidence to confront evil spirits, however they may show themselves, so that the peace of true religion may reign where it does not reign now.

March 18: Saint Cyril of Jerusalem, Bishop and Doctor

c. 315–386

Optional Memorial; Liturgical Color: Violet (Lenten Weekday)

A wise and persevering bishop teaches his flock

It is the Christ-given obligation of every Catholic bishop, and the priests and deacons who share in his ministry, to teach, sanctify, and govern all people under their spiritual care. Regarding teaching, the letters of Saint Paul, as well as the writings of early Christian theologians, abundantly attest to the duty of the Apostles and their appointed successors to ensure that false doctrine never infects their flocks. The episcopal duty to teach was not a charism or gift of the Holy Spirit such as speaking in tongues, performing miracles, or healing the infirm. Teaching correct doctrine might be aided by the Holy Spirit, but it was first a mandate from the Lord Himself. To not teach, to teach incompletely, or to teach falsely, was for the shepherd to ignore, neglect, or scatter the sheep entrusted to his care and protection.

Today's saint, Cyril, the Bishop of Jerusalem in the late fourth century, was a model teacher of right doctrine. He did not just teach teachers what to teach. He did not deputize or delegate others to teach on his behalf. He was the local Father, and, concerned for Christian formation in the household of faith, he personally taught the faith. How do we know this? Two reasons: First, because a holy woman named Egeria went on pilgrimage to Jerusalem in the 380s. She documented her travels in a journal identifying the bishop, known to be Cyril, as the catechist in the domed mausoleum covering the tomb of Christ (part of today's church of the Holy Sepulchre). Second, we know of Bishop Cyril's talks because many of them were dutifully recorded and preserved, presumably because of their high caliber. The talks are rich, early testimony to the perennial, consistent doctrines of the Catholic Church.

Egeria states that the bishop of Jerusalem taught about Lent and Easter to catechumens and neophytes (the newly baptized) by going through the entire Bible and the Creed, article by article. He taught for three hours each day, every one of the forty days of Lent and during Easter week. In his letter to the Romans, Saint Paul wrote, "But how are they to call on one in whom they have not believed? And how are they to believe in one of whom they have never heard? And how are they to hear without someone to proclaim him?" (Rm 10:14). Bishop Cyril admirably fulfilled his apostolic duty to teach and to proclaim so that others would know the Lord.

Among the profound teachings of Saint Cyril on the Mass, Baptism, and the Sacraments are his extended reflections on the nature of the Holy Eucharist. He is explicit: "Since He Himself has declared and said of the bread: This is My Body, who shall dare to doubt any more? And when He asserts and says: This is My Blood, who shall ever hesitate and say it is not His Blood?...Do not think it mere bread and wine, for it is the Body and Blood of Christ, according to the Lord's declaration" (St. Cyril Catechetical Lecture XXII). Cyril notes that if Christ could change water into wine, why could He not change wine into His own Blood? Reading these words of Cyril, it is perplexing that any modern Christian could doubt the real presence of Christ in the Holy Eucharist. As Saint John Henry Newman wrote: "To be deep in history is to cease to be a Protestant" (*An Essay on the Development of Christian Doctrine*, Introduction, Ch. 5).

Bishop Cyril was deeply involved in various consequential theological controversies of his day, was banished from Jerusalem, and participated in the First Council of Constantinople. He lived a long, complicated, and impactful life in the heart of the Church. He is in many ways a model to all bishops for his zealous yet tender care of souls, especially those preparing to be washed in the saving waters of baptism at Easter. Saint Cyril fortified the content of the Church's teaching with his personal presence, and by extension, the presence of the Sacrament of Holy Orders in his very person. He is a bishop remote in time, yet near in doctrine. Far removed from us historically, he is still close at our side when we stand to recite the same Creed he recited at every Sunday Mass.

Saint Cyril of Jerusalem, through your generous dedication to teaching the faith, come to the assistance of all catechists, ordained and lay, to be equally committed to teaching those under their care, in season and out of season, knowing that fidelity to the Lord and His Church is what counts the most.

March 19: Saint Joseph, Husband of the Blessed Virgin Mary

First Century

Solemnity; Liturgical Color: White

Patron Saint of the Universal Church, fathers, and a happy death

Jesus and Mary lived under his gentle, fatherly authority

The husband of Mary had a perfect spouse, untouched by original sin. He was also the foster father to a boy who was the Son of God and the Second Person of the Holy Trinity. Yet Saint Joseph, the least perfect member of his household, was still the head of the family. Authority does not always flow from moral or intellectual superiority. Authority in the Church, in particular, is God given. Because God chooses a certain person to fulfill a task in His household of faith, that person acts with a divine mandate to teach, sanctify, and govern the people and things entrusted to him. Saint Joseph is a model for how God uses imperfect instruments to exercise His perfect will. God does not want robots, machines, or zombies to mindlessly implement His plan for mankind. The history of the Church is replete with imperfect tools who have caused scandal and division. Wayward leaders have cost the Church entire countries. Yet despite all these unworthy instruments in the hands of the Divine Master, truth and shelter and grace continue to be provided to those baptised into the Church, the Master's family.

God wants personality. God wants us to have character. God's angels, created spirits, lack the restrictions imposed by a human body. But in not having a body, the angels also lack what makes us unique. They lack the spit, vinegar, and spark that make a man a man. Every man is an enfleshed soul, the coming together of a body and a spirit. This coming together is not half soul and half body, like the mythical centaur with the body of a horse but the torso and head of a man. When copper and zinc are welded together, they are superficially united into one larger piece of metal. But the union is not total and does not create something new. The copper is still copper, and the zinc is still zinc. But when copper and zinc are each melted down and then mixed together, they form brass. Brass is not just the joining of copper to zinc but an entirely new material with unique properties. In a similar way, the union of a body and a soul together composes a human person with unique properties, a child of God unlike any other. The saints, in particular, were unique people often possessing hot tempers, forceful personalities, and unbending wills. They placed their uniqueness at the service of God and His Church and helped to change the world. God did not make, and does not want, just vanilla ice cream. Everyone likes vanilla. But no one likes only vanilla. God wants flavor.

Saint Joseph was, like all the saints, unique. He probably had personal traits which were less than perfect. These imperfections were absolutely no obstacle to Mary and Jesus obeying him, loving him, and ceding to his authority in the Holy Family of Nazareth. Mary and Jesus would have happily bent to the will of their God-given guide, despite their metaphysical, moral, spiritual, and intellectual superiority.

Ancient traditions hold that Saint Joseph was considerably older than the Virgin Mary. Other traditions tell that he was married previously and that the "brothers" of Jesus were half-brothers from Saint Joseph's previous marriage. Scripture tells us Jesus was a carpenter and was known as the "carpenter's son" (Mt 13:55). Joseph may have been more precisely a builder who worked with the native stone so common to Palestinian construction. A Jewish ritual bath made of stone discovered beneath the church of Saint Joseph in Nazareth, a church which long tradition says was built over the Holy Family's home, may be Joseph's very own handiwork. A firm tradition teaches that Saint Joseph died long before his Son's death. This is based not on biblical evidence but on the lack of it. It can be reasonably presumed that Saint Joseph would have been present at his Son's crucifixion, as was Mary. Yet no mention is made of him being there. From this absence, biblical scholars have, from the beginning of the Church, surmised that Saint Joseph was

ST. JOSEPH

March 19

"Saint Joseph was a just man, a tireless worker, the upright guardian of those entrusted to his care. May he always guard, protect and enlighten families."

– Pope John Paul II

by then dead. Thus, Saint Joseph is the Patron Saint of a Happy Death, because he presumably died with Jesus and the Virgin Mary at his side. This is how all of us want to die, with Christ holding our hand on one side of the bed and the Virgin Mary seated beside us on the other side. Saint Joseph died in the best of company. May we do so as well.

Saint Joseph, Patron of the Universal Church, guide all those under the care of their pastors to see not their imperfections but their God-given obligation to fulfill God's plan. May your humble and faithful service inspire all fathers to lead their flocks with tenderness, wisdom, and strength.

March 23: Saint Turibius of Mogrovejo, Bishop

1538–1606

Optional Memorial; Liturgical Color: Violet (Lenten Weekday)

Patron Saint of Latin American Bishops and native people's rights

He died in the field six thousand miles from home

Today's saint was the second Archbishop of the second most important city in Spain's Latin American empire in the 1500s. Lima, Peru, stood only behind Mexico City in importance to the Spanish Crown during the pinnacle of its colonial ambitions. So when Lima's first Archbishop died in 1575, the King of Spain, not the Pope, searched for a suitable candidate to send over sea and land to replace him. The King found his man close at hand, and he was more than suitable to the task.

Turibius of Mogrovejo was a learned scholar of the law who held teaching and other posts in Spain's complex of Church and civil courts. Yet for all his learning, piety, faith, and energy, there was one huge obstacle to him being a bishop. Turibius was not a priest. He was not even a deacon. He was a very good, albeit unmarried, layman. The arrangement for centuries between Spain and the Holy See was that the Spanish Crown chose bishops while the Pope approved, or rejected, them. So after the Pope approved the appointment, over the candidate's fierce objections, Turibius received the four minor orders on four successive weeks, was ordained a deacon and then ordained a priest. He said his first Mass when he was over forty years old. About two years later, Turibius was consecrated as the new archbishop, and then sailed the ocean blue, arriving in Lima in May 1581.

Archbishop Turibius was extraordinarily dedicated to his episcopal responsibilities. He exhausted himself on years-long visits to the parishes of his vast territory, which included present day Peru and beyond. He acquainted himself with the priests and people under his care. He convoked synods (large Church meetings) to standardize sacramental, pastoral, and liturgical practice. He produced an important trilingual catechism in Spanish and two native dialects, learned to preach in these indigenous dialects himself, and encouraged his priests to be able to hear confessions and preach in them as well. Archbishop Turibius' life also providentially intersected with the lives of other saints active in Peru at the same time, including Martin de Porres, Francisco Solano, and Isabel Flores de Oliva, to whom Turibius gave the name Rose when he confirmed her. She was later canonized as Saint Rose of Lima, the first saint born in the New World. Saints know saints.

Archbishop Turibius was a fine example of a counter-reformation bishop, except that he did not serve in a counter-reformation place. That is, Peru was not split by the Catholic versus Protestant theological divisions wreaking such havoc in the Europe of that era. Saint Turibius implemented the reforms of the Council of Trent, not to combat heretics, but to simply make the Church healthier and holier, Protestants or no Protestants. From this perspective, the reforms of Trent were not a cure but an antidote. If Turibius' energy and holiness were motivated by any one thing besides evangelical fervor, it was his desire to make the Spanish colonists of Peru recover the integrity of their own baptisms. The indigenous population needed authentic examples of Christian living to respect and emulate, and few Spanish colonialists provided such models of right living. Saint Turibius' greatest enemy, then, was simply original sin, which returns to the battlefield every time a baby is born.

After exhausting himself through total dedication to his responsibilities, Saint Turibius fell ill on the road and died at age sixty-seven in a small town far from home. His twenty-four years as Archbishop were a trial of strength. He had baptized and confirmed half a million souls, had trekked thousands of miles on narrow paths made for goats, had never neglected to say Mass, and did not accept any gifts in return for what he gave. Turibius was canonized in 1726 and named the Patron Saint of Latin American Bishops by Pope Saint John Paul II in 1983. Perhaps his unforeseen ordination explains his sustained fervor and drive. What came late was valued for having come at all. He bloomed late and bloomed beautifully, becoming the Spanish equivalent of his great contemporary, the Italian Saint Charles Borromeo.

If a visitor searches for the tomb of the saintly Archbishop in the Cathedral of Lima today, he will not find it. There are only fragments of bones in a reliquary. His reputation for holiness was immediate and his relics were distributed far and wide after his death. He is in death as widely shared as he was in life, all the faithful wanting just a piece of the great man. In January 2018, Pope Francis prayed before the relics of Saint Turibius in Lima and invoked his memory in a talk to Peru's bishops. Saint Turibius did not, Pope Francis said, shepherd his diocese from behind a desk but was "a bishop with shoes worn out by walking, by constant travel, by setting out to preach the Gospel to all: to all places, on all occasions, without hesitation, reluctance, and fear."

Saint Turibius, we invoke your intercession to inspire all who share the gospel, in whatever form, to do so with ardor, skill, and charity, using all the means at their disposal, as you so powerfully did in your own life and ministry.

March 25: Annunciation of the Lord

Solemnity; Liturgical Color: White

The flutter of a wing, a rustling in the air, a voice, and the future began to begin

The Feast of the Annunciation is the reason why we celebrate Christmas on December 25. Christmas comes exactly nine months after the Archangel Gabriel invited the Virgin Mary to be the Mother of God, an event we commemorate on March 25. The dating of these Feast Days, although interesting, is of minor importance compared to their theological significance. It is fruitful to reflect upon the incarnation of Jesus Christ in the womb of the Virgin Mary as the antecedent to the explosion of joy, caroling, gift giving, eating, drinking, love and family unity that surrounds the birth of the Savior. Perhaps Mary had a sort of private and internal Christmas at the moment of the Annunciation. Maybe she felt the fullness of the world's Christmas joy inside of her own heart when she realized she had been chosen to be the Mother of God.

God could have become man in any number of creative ways. He could have incarnated Himself just as Adam was in the book of Genesis, by being formed from the clay and having the divine breath blown into his nostrils. Or God could have slowly backed down to earth on a tall golden ladder as a twenty-five-year-old man, ready to walk the highways and byways of Palestine. Or maybe God could have taken flesh in an unknown way and just been found, like Moses, floating in a basket by a childless young couple from Nazareth as they enjoyed a Sunday picnic along the Jordan River.

The Second Person of the Trinity chose, however, to become man like we all become man. In the same way that He would exit the world through the door of death before His Resurrection, as we all have to do, He also entered the world through the door of human birth. In the words of the early Church, Christ could not redeem what He did not assume. He redeemed everything because He took on human nature in all of its breadth, depth, complexity and mystery. He was like us in all things save sin.

The incarnation of the Second Person of the Trinity was a self-emptying. It was God becoming small. Imagine a man becoming an ant while retaining his human mind and will. The man-turned-ant would appear to be like all the ants around him, and would participate in all of their ant activities, yet still think at a level far above them. There was no other way to do it. The man had to learn through becoming, not because insect life was superior to his own, but because it was inferior. Only through descending, only through experience, could the man learn what was below him. All analogies limp, but, in a similar way, the Second Person of the Trinity retained His infused divine knowledge while reducing Himself to a man and learning man life, doing man work, and dying a man death. By such a self-emptying, He dignified all men and opened to them the possibility of entering into His higher life in Heaven.

The Annunciation
John William Waterhouse

The Church's tradition speculates that one reason the bad angels may have rebelled against God was the besetting sin of envy. They may have discovered that God chose to become man instead of the higher form of an angel. This envy would have been directed at the Virgin Mary as well, that Vessel of Honor and Ark of the Covenant who bore the divine choice. God not only became man, we must remember, but did so through a human being, one prepared from her conception to be perfect. March 25 is one of only two days of the year when we kneel at the recitation of the Creed at Mass. At the words "...by the Holy Spirit was incarnate of the Virgin Mary and became man" all heads bow and all knees bend at the wonder of it. If the story of Christ is the greatest story ever told, today is its first page.

O Holy Virgin Mary, we ask your intercession to make us as generous as you in accepting the will of God in our lives, especially when that will is expressed in mysterious ways. May you be our example of a generous response to what God desires of us.

LENT, HOLY WEEK & MOVEABLE FEASTS

"Reach out your hand and put it in my side. Do not doubt but believe." Jn 20:27

The Incredulity of Saint Thomas
Michelangelo Merisi da Caravaggio

Ash Wednesday

Forty-six days before Easter
Liturgical Color: Violet

Without God we are a tiny pile of crumbs

The marauding pirates of the high seas had their tough skin inked with tattoos. Roman soldiers smothered their bodies in oil before a battle. Primitive peoples ritually paint a warrior's face before a fight, stretch earlobes with hoops, or pierce noses with large rings. When American Indians wanted to emulate the ferocity or speed of an animal, a sharp bone fragment was used to carve that creature's outline into their skin, where it was stained with dye or soot. Traditionally, when a simple man wanted to announce what tribe he ran with, what nation he would die for, or what woman he would defend, he didn't need to say a word. He just lifted up his shirt a bit, rolled up his sleeve, or pointed to a mark on his neck. Clothes, hairstyle, and cosmetics communicate status, origin, belonging, and commitment well. But they can all be removed or changed. Tattoos, scalpings, piercings, brands, paints, and scars use the body as their canvas to permanently convey what words cannot.

On Ash Wednesday, Catholics receive a temporary ash "tattoo" of a cross just above their eyes and nose. This primal gesture evokes the raw, uncomplicated, religious devotion at the core of our otherwise sophisticated theology. The Church consecrates the body externally with water and oil in Baptism, Confirmation, and Anointing of the Sick. The Church reads Saint Thomas Aquinas, sings refined Latin chant, and prays before luminous stained glass. And it also smudges black ashes on our faces. Real religions do things like this. A real religion has priests who smear your face with dirty ash as they whisper, "You're gonna die."

Man's earthly end, the separation of soul and body, could have come about in many ways. But due to original sin, this end always comes through death. Death is a punishment for Adam and Eve's sin of pride in eating the fruit of the Tree of Knowledge of Good and Evil in the Garden of Eden. This sin is not original in the sense of being authentic or unrepeatable, but in that it occurred at our common origin. As a permanent repercussion of His punishment, God made work burdensome and instituted death as the mysterious doorway through which all must walk to exit earthly life. God told this to our common parents in Genesis 3:19: "By the sweat of your face you shall eat bread until you return to the ground, for out of it you were taken; you are dust, and to dust you shall return." The last of these words are repeated to the faithful as the ashes are placed on their foreheads on Ash Wednesday.

But as these words of death and destruction, of returning to the ground, are spoken, the priest does not trace an ash circle or a black question mark on our foreheads. He traces a cross. In this sign we shall conquer. In no other sign will we conquer. So with death comes a promise. With the old Adam there comes a new Adam—Jesus Christ. This is how Jesus was first understood in the early Church. Mary was the New Eve. Christ was the New Adam. They untied the knot our remote ancestors had tied. They were faithful where Adam and Eve were unfaithful. They kept the promise Adam and Eve had broken.

The start of the forty days of Lent is a practice run. One day, we will all have to give an accounting of our lives. The balance sheet will have to be settled, the good and the bad weighed in their columns. Ash Wednesday is a reminder of something we know but don't call to mind often enough. Without God all that remains of our greatness is a little pile of dust. We are, in a sense, marked with ourselves today. The tiny black crumbs of ash will fall away in a matter of hours, to be forgotten for another year. And life will go on. Such is our destiny. With God, everything. Without God, nothing.

God of all, we ask that we live a fruitful Lent starting on this Ash Wednesday. Help us to be faithful to our promises of penance, sacrifice, and repentance for past sins. May we see in the ashes of today our true nature without You. May we see in the cross our true destiny with You.

Palm Sunday of the Passion of the Lord

c. 33 A.D.

The Sunday before Easter

Solemnity; Liturgical Color: Red

Beginning with the end we understand His greatness

One way to understand a book, or to watch a movie, is to begin at the end. To read, or watch, backwards allows every character and plot twist to be interpreted in light of their conclusions. Working backwards removes much of the drama and tension from a story, of course, but it also makes the story perfectly intelligible. No slow unwinding of the plot, no "whodunit," no surprise around the corner, and no unexpected deaths. Skipping to the end makes the entire narrative clear, with prior knowledge infusing prior meaning into the story as it unfolds.

The Gospels of Matthew, Mark, Luke, and John are essentially Passion narratives with extended introductions. There is plenty of evidence that the end of Christ's life, particularly his last seventy-two hours, were well remembered by His disciples, the events being repeated in great detail until they were ultimately written down. The Evangelists eventually supplemented these often-repeated Passion narratives with further details about Christ's life which had occurred long before Holy Week. These prior narratives are often inconsistent across the Gospels, emphasize diverse aspects of Christ's life, and omit or add details in a seemingly arbitrary manner. What are very consistent, however, are the Passion narratives. Their vivid details are, without doubt, the heart and soul of the story of Jesus Christ.

On Palm Sunday we begin with the end. We read our way backwards. It is not possible for any Christian to think of Jesus Christ divorced from how His earthly life ended. Even the earliest Christian writings were composed from a post-Resurrection perspective. The "real" Jesus of history did not have miracles placed on Him like ornaments on a Christmas tree. His miracles were not later adornments hung on His human frame to lend Him credibility. The "real" Jesus is not the simple carpenter lurking in the shadows behind the Christ of Faith created by later generations. There are scant biblical references to Jesus' occupation as a carpenter, or to

His simple and humble existence in a provincial town. There is a massive amount of biblical evidence, on the contrary, that Jesus suffered, died, and rose from the dead. And this biblical evidence is buttressed by an abundance of postbiblical testimony and the universal witness of an army of Apostles, saints, and martyrs.

All of this means that the "real" Jesus is the Christ of faith! The "real" Jesus did suffer, die, and rise from the dead! The "real" Jesus is not found in the *subtext* of the Gospels—He is found in the *text* of the Gospels! And those texts are indisputably ancient. In other words, the narrative read at Mass on Palm Sunday is the oldest, truest, and most well-remembered portion of one of the most fully preserved and extraordinary documents from the ancient world—the New Testament.

Our faith is rooted in history, a miraculous history. The Passion of Jesus Christ is not a parable, analogy, or metaphor. It is not a story meant to teach us a lesson apart from its facts. It is not a morality play whose actors mean to teach a lesson. The Passion of Christ is theologically significant because it is historically true. If it were not historically true, it would have no significance beyond its power to inspire as a story. But every culture already has myths to inspire its people, or at least mythical figures whose superhuman qualities model greatness. The story of Christ is so much more. It is the true story of a God-man who was betrayed by a friend, suffered calumny from His enemies, was publicly humiliated, made to carry the instrument of His own execution, and then was left to die, naked on a rough-hewn tree.

This story is not sad by analogy to another story. It is sad in and of itself. This is the story we hear every Palm Sunday. This is how a great man's life came to an end. It is also the story of how the Son of God conquered death and opened the gates of heaven to all who not only believe in Him but who belong to Him through the Catholic Church.

Lord of the Passion, You suffered calumny and humiliation, You bore the Cross and did not complain. Intercede before Your heavenly Father that we may bear whatever crosses we must with fortitude. Without Your grace, we are no better than Godless pagans, in search of frivolous signs to lend meaning to life.

Thursday of Holy Week (Holy Thursday)

c. 33 A.D.

Triduum; Liturgical Color: White

No last will and testament has been as heeded as Christ's

From the moment Christ first uttered the words at the Last Supper on Holy Thursday evening, the Church has never ceased to be faithful to them: "Do this in memory of me." These words of a man about to die, if not a dying man, were a commandment more than a request, marching orders more than a mission statement. And everyone in that upper room understood exactly what He meant. No last will and testament of any man has ever been as faithfully fulfilled as these last words of Christ. What Christ ordered to be done has been done, and continues to be done, every day, throughout the world, by every single priest who stands at an altar and recites the words of consecration *in persona Christi*.

The world has never moved on from Christ and never will. He is not in the world's rear-view mirror. He is here, He is present, He is alive. And in every tight corner of the globe, from a tidy Polish village to a rambling Filipino city, from a Palestinian monastery hugging a sun-baked cliff to an Argentinian parish in a sprawling suburb, the Mass makes Him real because it is done in memory of Him. Literally every minute of every day, Mass is celebrated across the globe in a ceaseless offering to God the Father. "From the rising of the sun to its setting," in a thousand tongues, priests bend slightly over their chalices and the white linens covering their altars and carefully repeat a chain of words in a cadence known to all the faithful: "Take this, all of you, and eat of it…Take this all of you, and drink from it…This is my Body…This is my Blood." No words are more familiar. None! Not Shakespeare's, not Caesar's, not Lincoln's. The everlasting words of the cross-cultural and cross-generational Christ simply have no equal.

If we expect from the Church the sacraments, we will never be disappointed. If we receive from the Church more than the sacraments, we should rejoice. The Last Supper fulfills and completes the Jewish Passover sacrifice ordered by God of Moses and the Jews in Egypt. The Last Supper, at the same time, prefigures in an unbloody way the physical sacrifice Christ would make on the morrow on the hill of Calvary. In the Last Supper, Christ also gives priests the perennial form for the Holy Sacrifice of the Mass. The Last Supper, then, is a composite act of Jewish and Christian ritual, of Old and New Testament theology, of historical and spiritual realities all packed into one dense liturgical act which the Church presents anew at every Mass. The Mass is the Christian work of art *par excellence.* It is the public act which never stops showing. It is the magnet which pulls mankind through the doors of thousands of churches every morning, noon, and night.

We do this in memory of Him because God deserves worship as a matter of justice, not charity. We do this in memory of Him because He ordered us to do so. We do this in memory of Him because it prefigures what we will hopefully do in heaven for eternity. And we do this in memory of Him for a thousand million reasons locked in the quiet places of a thousand million hearts: For Jill to come back home. So that Robert survives the war. In thanksgiving for a good husband. So that a pain in the gut not be what it might be. In gratitude for the rain that saved the crops. At a king's crowning, a convict's death, or the bond of marriage. For the shocked just after the martyrs' mangled bodies were dragged out of the arena over the blood-stained sand. In thanksgiving because my father did not die of cancer, and in remembrance of my cousin who did. For the fireman who couldn't find his way out of the building, for the barren woman, for the anniversary of an aged couple, or for the nation on its birthday. There is no end of reasons.

Month after month, year after year, century after century, until the sands of time run out, the voice of the Lord on Holy Thursday echoes over the waters and down the halls of time: "Do this in memory of me." *

Lord Jesus Christ, Your total physical gift of self on Good Friday began internally at the Last Supper. May the faithful often profit from Your priestly ministry by receiving Your body and blood consecrated on Your sacred altars by those who share in Your one priesthood.

**See "The Shape of the Liturgy" by Dom Gregory Dix for a similar reflection on the Holy Eucharist.*

Friday of the Passion of the Lord (Good Friday)

c. 33 A.D.

Triduum; Liturgical Color: Red

No one knew love looked like this

One of the most famous Greek sculptures in the world, a larger-than-life marble statue of a female, reigns over a monumental staircase in the Louvre. A soft, unfelt breeze ripples through the thin, flowing sheets that wrap her frame. Two expansive, articulated wings sweep elegantly back from her torso, giving the impression that she has just floated down from on high and landed softly on the prow of an invisible ship. Though now headless, the statue's sense of movement is so vivid that one can still "see" her neck craning, her jaw jutting, and her eyes looking carefully downward as she settles to ground. She moves and yet she is still. She is "Winged Victory," Nike, the Greek goddess of victory.

Victory in battle, conquest in war, and success in sport are typically celebrated with a blast of trumpets, gold medals hung around the neck, ticker-tape parades, a crowning with laurels, or the placing of an elegant statue like "Winged Victory" to serenely personify triumph over one's enemies. Jesus Christ changed all that. He changed what victory looked like. Jesus climbed a different podium to win a different type of victory over man's greatest enemy.

On Good Friday, the God of the Living descended into the depths of human experience to conquer death. His victory parade was the carrying of the Cross on His tender shoulders up the hill of Calvary, where His hands were nailed to a splintery timber. He was raised on high by centurions for mockery, not exaltation. He then died a slow, agonizing death as His thorax sunk lower and lower and His diaphragm sucked less and less air into His lungs. It was not fast and clean. It took three hours. No one knew it at the time, but this was the new look of love in the Christian age, this was the new victory pose. Not laurels, but thorns. Not trumpets, but screams. Not medals, but scars. On Good Friday, Christ redefined victory. The victor is not prideful or strong, but humble, meek, wrecked, injured, and dead. Pain in the non-Christian world, whether in the past or today, has no redemptive power or reward. It is just mindless

Deposition from the Cross
Luca Cambiaso

(Städel Museum, Frankfurt am Main)

and arbitrary suffering. At best, it is stoicism. In the person of Jesus Christ, God does not explain human suffering. Instead, He gives it meaning. And giving meaning to something is a type of answer, although not a solution. We do not go to a funeral to solve a problem. We go simply to be present, to share the family's sorrow. Sharing is a powerful response. It is more satisfying and profound to give something meaning than to make it disappear. The answer of Jesus Christ to human suffering is to share it. His answer is empathy. He suffers, dies, and is buried. No one can point a finger at God and say, "You don't know what it's like!" He certainly does know what it's like! Jesus could have saved the world by cutting Himself shaving. But He didn't. He experienced more than was necessary, because it was more fitting that God share every single human experience except sin. God drinks the common cup of human suffering to the dregs.

Jesus did not die full of years. He died young, like many tragic heroes. Christ's death gives hope to all who are preyed upon by loneliness, depression, fear, illness, anxiety, confusion, sin, and shame. In His death, Jesus does not just tell us but shows us that all these things can be conquered when united to Him. Jesus did not leave us a book but a life. And that life continues to be shared with us in word and sacrament, in its fullness, in the Catholic Church.

God did not die on the Cross so that artists could sculpt Him. God died for a higher reason. He died for us. In Christ, the gift and the giver, the priest and the sacrifice, merge, and the result is life. As in marriage, so also in the Trinity, self-gift merges in generative love and creates life. So we etch that powerful reminder of Christ's life-generating gift of self—the Crucifix—into our tombstones and place it high in our churches. This universal symbol of redemptive love even hangs from fine chains on our necks. *In hoc signo vinces.* Christ is our new winged Victory, not with two glorious wings spreading out in a proud gesture of triumph, but with His two thin bloody arms pinned to the Cross. He hangs there in agony, gasping for air, and heroically waits for Sunday to come.

Crucified Lord, in Your passion and death, You walked for us the hard path to new life. You exited life through the door of death and so give us hope that the end is the beginning, that loss is gain, that defeat is victory, and that death is life.

The Resurrection
Cecco del Caravaggio

(Art Institute of Chicago)

Easter Sunday of the Resurrection of the Lord

c. 33 A.D.

The first Sunday after the first full moon that falls on, or after, March 21

Solemnity; Liturgical Color: White or Gold

Checkmate!

If you want to discover what's really going on in a story, follow the women. Curious about how the plot of a book, movie, or show is going to resolve itself? Follow the female characters, because the men...and the rest of the story...will soon catch up with them. It is a female disciple, Mary Magdalen, who takes our hand and walks us quickly onto the stage of Easter Sunday. Mary doesn't go to the tomb on Saturday, because no work can be done on the Sabbath. So early Sunday, while it is still dark, Mary walks alone to the burial garden and sees something, or, more precisely, doesn't see something, that changes world history. The dead body of Jesus is not on the slab! The stone is rolled away! The tomb is empty! Mary Magdalen is witness one, the first of billions to know that Jesus rose from the dead. Witness one then quickly runs to tell the good news to witness two and three, the Apostles Peter and John. Thus the first links in the endless chain of believers were forged, a strong, enduring chain that has wended its way through history until today.

Relegating Jesus' miracles to the bin of apocryphal but consoling stories, many moderns argue Christ's most enduring legacy is the verifiable good He did for His fellow men. Yet the Gospels don't tell us that Jesus went around doing good. They tell us He went around doing miracles. Jesus doesn't help an old woman carry a load up a hill. He doesn't dig His hand deep into His pocket and spare some change. Jesus doesn't offer words of comfort to the sick; He heals the sick. Jesus doesn't jump into the sea to save the drowning Peter; He walks on the water. Jesus didn't volunteer in a soup kitchen; He miraculously multiplied bread and fish and distributed food to the masses. And Jesus didn't save people from the danger of death; He raised them from the dead. Jesus temporarily resuscitated three people, all of whom later died, before He resurrected Himself forever. There was nothing dreamy about the Resurrection. Real people with real names in a real place saw the Resurrected Jesus with real eyes. Easter celebrates the miracle of all miracles, the greatest unexpected result of all time, the indispensable genesis event of Western Civilization.

So today we raise a toast to a fresh spring morning two thousand years ago. In a garden moist with dew, with small birds chirping and flowers' bending toward the dawning sun, in a small, darkened hollow cut into the rock, a dead man, icy cold to the touch, zapped to life. He achingly rose from His stone slab and walked slowly toward the low entrance. He rolled away a heavy stone and stepped out into a new world where death was no longer the master. The ageless, see-saw battle between life and death was resolved in favor of the more powerful. Checkmate! The mind wanders at the beauty of it all.

The story is told of the conception of twins. In their first weeks of life they stretch and groan and grow. They are happy to be alive, to be together. They squirm and jostle and explore their cramped watery world. They are curious. They see a life cord tethering them to someone greater and are overjoyed. "How great is our mother's love that she shares her life with us." Weeks turn into months in their warm amniotic bath. The twins shift and change. "What does this mean?" Twin One asks. "It means that our life in the womb is ending," Twin Two responds. "But I don't want to leave the womb! I am happy here. I want to stay here forever, close to our mother!" "But we have no choice," Twin Two responds again. "Besides, maybe...just maybe, there is life after birth." Twin One: "But how can that be? The sac will break, the cord will be severed, and we'll be cut off from our source of life. And besides, there's evidence that others were here before us, and none has ever come back to tell us that there is life after birth. No, this is the end." Twin Two begins to despair, "If life in the womb ends in death, what's its purpose? It's meaningless! Maybe...maybe we don't even have a mother...maybe we just made her up." Twin One: "But we must have a mother. How else did we get here? How else do we stay alive?"

And so the last days in the womb were filled with questioning and deep fear about the future. The moment of birth came at an hour they did not expect. The twins were emotional, wondering about the unknown, uncertain if they would ever see each other, or their mother, again. The transition was painful. They struggled. They heard screams. All that they knew disappeared. And then… light! Shocking bright whiteness. Their eyelids slowly peeled from their skin, and they gazed in confused wonder at a new world around them. Their life-source, their great mother, wept when they were placed in her arms. They could feel her love radiating into them. The twins were in an unknown world that calmed every fear, that exceeded their wildest dreams. Their eyes had not seen and their ears had not heard anything like this before. Their end was just their beginning. They were overcome and could do only one thing—cry out for joy.

Risen Lord, strengthen our faith so that we overcome all doubt, and place our trust in Your gift of life beyond the grave. May Your resurrection from the dead inflame in us an ardent desire to be holy in this life so that we can live with You, Mary, and all the saints in the next.

Second Sunday of Easter (Divine Mercy Sunday)

Solemnity; Liturgical Color: White

True power pardons

In the Nicene Creed, we say that Jesus is seated at the right hand of the Father. When a judge walks into a courtroom, the bailiff announces, "All rise," and the judge sits in judgment. In his see city, a bishop rests in his *cathedra*, and in his palace, a king reigns from his throne. A president signs legislation while seated at his desk. The chair is a locus of power. The power that emanates from such seats of authority judges, condemns, and sentences. Today's feast reminds us, though, that authority also exercises power by granting mercy. When a judge pronounces innocence, the sentence is no less binding than one of guilt. The absolved exits the court into a new day, ready to begin again. And when the priest's voice whispers through the screen, "I absolve you from your sins in the name of the Father, the Son, and the Holy Spirit," guilt evaporates into thin air. The purest and truest expression of power is the granting of mercy.

Mercy is a superabundance of justice, not an exception to it. When faced with a wound to the common good, those responsible for repairing the damage do not have two contrary options: justice or mercy. Justice and mercy are not mutually exclusive. Mercy is a form of justice. Mercy does not ignore the tears to the fabric of the common good slashed by crime and sin. Rightful authority notes the torn fabric, weighs the personal responsibility of the accused, and distributes justice precisely by granting mercy. Mercy does not turn a blind eye to justice but fulfills its obligations to justice by going beyond them. After all, one cannot be absolved of having done nothing. Similarly, where there is no guilt there is no need of mercy. When justice calls out, two words echo back off the hard walls: "condemnation" and "mercy." Mercy runs parallel to, and beyond, the path of condemnation. This is the mercy we celebrate today, the mercy whose greatest practitioner is God Himself. Because He is the seat of all authority, God is also the seat of all mercy.

God plays many roles in the life of the Christian—Creator, Savior, Sanctifier, and Judge. Our Creed teaches us that God the Son, seated at the Father's right hand, "will come in glory to judge the living and the dead," both at the particular and at the final judgment. At that moment, it will serve us nothing to state, in excusing our sins, that "God understands." Of course God understands. To state "God understands" is just another way to say that God is omniscient and all powerful. "God understands" implies that because God knows the powerful temptations of the world, the flesh, and the devil, that He could not possibly judge man harshly. Yet "God understands" is a lazy manner of exculpating sinful behavior. When nose to nose with God one second after death, the repentant Christian should plead, instead, "Lord, have mercy." Faced with the scandalous behavior of a friend or relative, the response should again be "Lord, have mercy." Appealing to God's mercy will melt His heart. Appealing to His knowledge will not.

The private revelations of Jesus Christ to Saint Faustina Kowalska, a Polish nun and intense mystic who died in 1938, are the source of the profound spirituality of today's feast. Sister Faustina was a kind of Saint Catherine of Siena of the twentieth century. She lived a regimen of fasting, meditation, liturgical prayer, and close community life that would have crushed a less resilient soul. But Faustina persevered, amidst debilitating illnesses, sisterly jealousy, and respectful but questioning superiors. Her diaries are replete with the starkest of language from the mouth of Christ, showing that moral clarity precedes the call for mercy. Sister Faustina faithfully recorded Christ's manly commands in her diary. One of these commands expressly desired that the Divine Mercy be celebrated on the Sunday after Easter. In an age-old pattern familiar to an ancient Church, Saint Faustina's private revelations were challenged, filtered for theological truth, sifted for spiritual depth, and granted universal approbation by the only Christian religion which even claims to grant such. In the soundest proof of their authenticity, the profound simplicity of the Divine Mercy revelations and of their related devotions were intuitively grasped

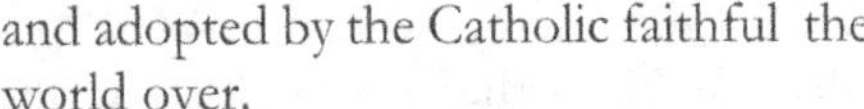
and adopted by the Catholic faithful the world over.

Pope Saint John Paul II first inserted today's feast into the Roman calendar on April 30, 2000, the canonization day of Saint Faustina. John Paul II was also canonized on Divine Mercy Sunday in 2014. And so the Church's third millennium was launched with a new devotion that quickly eclipsed many older ones, a new piety rooted in the most ancient truths, a fresh appeal to a side of God that had not been fully understood in prior ages. Divine Mercy is the new face of God for the third millennium, a postmodern Sacred Heart. This is the God who leans in and waits with bated breath for us to whisper through the screen, "Forgive me, Father, for I have sinned." This is the God who at the end of time, whether our own time or all time, waits to hear from our lips those few prized words "Lord, have mercy." Having heard that, He need not hear anything more. And having received that, we need not receive anything more.

Divine Mercy, do not hold our sins against us. Be a merciful Father who judges us in the fullness of Your power, punishing when needed, but granting mercy when we need it more, most especially when we are too saturated with pride to request it.

Made in the USA
Monee, IL
10 August 2024